The Whirl

by "Dr. Sue."

and Other Things that Women Do

Illustrations by Tim Pritchard (www.tims-toons.com)

Walnut Springs Press
110 South 800 West
Brigham City, Utah 84302
Http://walnutspringspress.blogspot.com

ISBN: 978-1-935217-32-9

The Girl in a Whirl by "Dr. Sue," and Other Things that Women Do

Random & Quirky Poems for Women on Being LDS, Family Stuff, & This & That About Life

Victoria Gunther

Acknowledgments

My love and endless appreciation go to my husband, Jay, who insisted that I stop anything else and write this book, then did 100% of everything at home so I could. You're my best friend and the love of my life. To my children: Being your mother has been one of my greatest blessings, even though "being the mommy" all these years has pretty much worn me out! I love that you all are kind and caring, and I'm proud of you. You've also provided me with endless stories to write about! Thanks also to our sweet daughters-in-law for being part of us. I admire you both.

Thank you, Jill Taylor, for knowing the perfect thing to do. None of this would have happened without you.

A huge thanks to my editor, Linda Prince. You were amazingly insightful and helpful! Thanks to Scot and Maurine Proctor at MeridianMagazine.com for running the original The Girl in a Whirl, which opened many doors for me. And to the incredibly sweet and funny Joni Hilton for your generous kindness.

My thanks to Merrilee Boyack for your example, endless enthusiasm, and constant willingness to bless others, including me. My sincere thanks to Tim Pritchard, our cartoonist. You were a pleasure to work with, start to finish.

Thank you, Jack Weyland, for the goodness you brought into our teens' lives, and for your personal kindness to me as I was getting this book out. I'm very grateful.

My lifelong gratitude to Haws Marble for teaching me to love the scriptures, the late John Young for teaching me to love and follow the living prophets, and John Lund for teaching me how to seek the Lord.

Foreword

Life can be very, very serious. But our attitude toward life certainly doesn't have to be! Vitamin H—humor—can prevent everything from dull hair to dull personalities! Taken in regular doses, humor can bring vitality into any day, inject joy in any cloud, and cause us to look at our lives with hope and happiness.

The Girl in the Whirl will give you a HUGE dose of vitamin H and can be reapplied as needed. I loved it so much that I began reading it to my husband. Normally, he hates this but he actually stayed and listened because he loved it too! Now THAT is the sign of a great book! There are so many pearls of wisdom and simple yet important truths taught here with love and great humor.

What's not to love about lessons that include toothbrushes, JELL-O, trampolines, and the care for deceased pets? After reading about the snake (I shall not spoil the surprise), I didn't feel so bad about the foot-tall plant I discovered growing out of the drain of my sons' bathtub. Because our lives may include the weird and the wacky, vitamin H is part of our survival kit!

Along with the joy of humor, this book will also touch your heart as it moves you from tears of laughter to tears of understanding. I give *The Girl in a Whirl* two thumbs up! Well, my hubby loved it too, so that's FOUR thumbs up!!

To sum up my praises for this book, I channeled my inner poet:

I love it! I love it!
Oh this much is true.
You just have to read this,
Until it is through!

The Girl in a Whirl might bring out the poet in *you* too!

May you enjoy a life full of healthy fiber, organic chocolate (is there such a thing?), and rich doses of vitamin H supplied by the good-humor woman, Victoria Gunther!

Merrilee Boyack

The Girl in a Whirl

by "Dr. Sue"

"Look at me, look at me, look at me now!
You could do what *I* do if you only knew how.
I study the scriptures one hour each day.
I bake and I garden. I scrub and I pray.

I always keep all the commandments completely.
I speak to my little ones gently and sweetly.
I help in their classrooms! I sew all they wear!
I drive them to practice! I cut all their hair!

I memorize talks by the General Authorities.
I focus on things to be done by priorities.
I keep our home organized, clean, and attractive.
I drop by with goodies and see the less active.

I play the piano! I bless with my talents!
My toilets all sparkle! My checkbooks all balance!
Each week every child gets a one-on-one date.
I attend all my meetings (on time! Never late!)

I'm taking a class on the teachings of Paul,
But that is not all! Oh, no. That is not all . . .

I track my bad habits 'til each is abolished.
I floss every day! And my toenails are polished!
Our family home evenings are always delightful.
The lessons I give are both fun and insightful.

I do genealogy faithfully, too.
It's easy to do all the things that I do!
I rise each day early, refreshed, and awake.
I've learned all the names of the youth in my stake!

I read to my children! I help all my neighbors!
I bless the community, too, with my labors.
I write in my journal! I sing in the choir!
Each day, I write "thank you's" to those I admire.

I exercise and I cook menus gourmet.
My visiting teaching is done the first day!
(I also go do it for someone who missed hers.
I love filling in for my cherished ward sisters.)

I chart resolutions and check off each goal.
I seek each "lost lamb" on my Primary roll.
I bottle our produce each summer and fall.
But that is not all! Oh, no. That is not all . . .

I went back to school to update my degree.
My studying earned me a new Ph.D.
I split with the sisters who cover our ward
To spread the glad truth that the gospel's restored.

I go to the temple at least once a week.
I make my girls' prom dresses—modest, yet chic.
My sons were all Eagles when they were fourteen!
My kids get straight A's! And their bedrooms are clean!

I have my own business to help earn some money.
I always look beautifully groomed for my honey.
I grind my own wheat and I bake all our bread.
I plan our nutritious meals six months ahead.

I make sure I rotate our two-year's supply.
My shopping for Christmas is done by July!
(It's out of the way early on for a reason.
I then can prepare for the *real* Christmas season.)

These things are not hard. It is good if you do them.
You can if you try! Set goals and pursue them!
It's easy to do all the things that I do!
If you plan and work smart, you can do them all too!

It's easy!" she said.

And then . . .

. . . she dropped dead.

Yep. Sadly, she kicked the bucket. Well, *she* probably kicked the mop bucket. I guess we can't say she bit the dust, because you know that wherever she's been, there wouldn't be one single speck of dust left for her to bite, right? But whether she kicked or bit or what, she's gone. And you know why? Because it's impossible for *anyone* to do all those things at one time, and that includes the Girl in a Whirl!

We just *think* it probably should be possible. And even though we aren't quite able to do all that yet, deep down, we seem to believe that somewhere out there, other women somehow are.

Well, I have an important news flash for you: Any woman like the Girl in a Whirl ONLY exists on the unreality TV shows of the Pamela Perfect Utopia Channel. I know you've probably heard highly reliable rumors of a not-too-distant ward where she actually lives and breathes, working organizational miracles on a daily basis. But the woman is *just a myth,* despite your firsthand knowledge that your visiting teacher's sister-in-law's manicurist knows her well, and can vouch for her ongoing perfectitude.

Okay, hopefully, that takes care of *her,* then. But here's the real question. Oh, sisters, why do we feel like we need to be like that, anyway? Why do we feel guilty, or second-rate, or like we're just not good enough despite what we *do,* because of everything we *don't* manage to do? It's like we have this demented little alarm system in the back of our brains screaming, "In order to be good enough, I need to do and be everything that anyone might possibly expect of me, plus work on every single one of life's vitally important issues and purposes—all TODAY!"

Well, I have another news flash for you, and it's a real one this time. In fact, it's *the* good news—the best news in all of eternity. Because of our Heavenly Father's plan of happiness (isn't it so sweet how Alma calls it that?), and what our Savior did for us, He can make sure we are definitely good enough. Perfect, in fact. Sounds hard to believe, doesn't it? But that IS what it says right here in Moroni 10:32:

> *Yea, come unto Christ, and be perfected in him, and deny yourselves of all ungodliness; and if ye shall deny yourselves of all ungodliness, and love God with all your might, mind and strength, then is his grace sufficient for you, that by his grace ye may be perfect in Christ; and if by the grace of God ye are perfect in Christ, ye can in nowise deny the power of God.*

When we break this down, it's an invitation for us to come to Christ and let His grace make us PERFECT in Him, which, by the way, is *way* different than the kind of "perfect" some of us think of when we hear the word. This one is something we can actually do! When we really look at the things Moroni talks about there, we realize that they're so completely doable—nothing like all the crazy stuff that goes on in our heads about what all we *think* we supposedly have to be and do.

Okay, so here's what Moroni counsels us to do:

1. Come to Christ: *Not hard.* Just learning about what

He's truly like is enough to make you want to do that anyway.

2. Deny yourself of all ungodliness: Well, that might take a little bit of trying, depending on the circumstances. But who *wants* all that crud, anyway? Really, once you start to pull away from things that are ungodly, unholy, unclean, and all, it feels soooooo much better. It's sort of like you were having what you thought was a nice, little swim, but when someone helps you out and you look back, you see that you were actually swimming in the sewer. Eeew! Once you've climbed out and are far enough away to really see it, you recognize that it's nothing worth going back to.
3. Love God: This one is easy. Heavenly Father is kind, good, merciful, just, powerful, loves you more than anything, and is Someone you can trust completely, since He will make all things work together for your good. (And no, that doesn't mean nothing hard or "bad" ever happens. It just means He will use it to bless your life in one way or another.)
4. Number 4? What's number 4? Is there SUPPOSED to be a number 4? Oh. I guess not. Well, that's it then. Just three little items on the list and that's all!

Now, here's the point I'd like to make about all this. It's that you can stop worrying or being stressed or depressed or demotivated or fearful or whatever it is you get, over how much you can't do. You can come to Christ. He is so loving and kind. He just wants you to start right where you are and come, as it says so simply in this part of one of my favorite scriptures: "Whosoever *will* come, *may* come" (Alma 42:27; emphasis added). You don't need to worry about whether or not He'll accept you. He will. The only question is if *you* will go to *Him*.

Once you do, He'll even help you work on the next part, which is denying yourself of all ungodliness. That's also something you can do. And you'll be so glad once you do! That will open up all kinds of possibilities to you that you don't have now, mainly through the constant companionship of the Holy Ghost. And if that doesn't sound very exciting, that's okay, because just wait until you try out how it feels. Incredible. The best thing ever. Seriously. And one day pretty soon here, you're going to think back on this and say, "Wow! That was really the truth! I had no idea this was so amazing." So yes, you can deny yourself all ungodliness and you will *want* to.

If you need help understanding what any ungodliness in your life might be, you could check out some simple standards in *For the Strength of Youth*. Although it is written for the youth, in our stake, our leaders spent a year discussing it with the stake. They called it *For the Strength of YOU*, meaning *all* of us, since it contains basic standards for those who desire to be pure in heart and in action. If you need more help, or maybe even better help, ask your Heavenly Father. If you really want to know what you should do about your life right now and where you should start, He's the best one to ask. He not only knows you perfectly, but He's *so* wonderful to work with. He won't overwhelm you with 387 things you need to do right now. Typically, if you ask Him that question, you will most likely feel a gentle "pressing" within your heart or have a thought that will make you consider something you should stop doing, that you already knew anyway, at which point, you will say, "So, how do I know this isn't just me?" Well, it probably isn't just you, because when you ask Heavenly Father sincerely, He is glad that you want to repent, and He is happy to answer you. However, sometimes when you already clearly know something, that *is* the answer, and you really do need to start working on that. You know it and He knows it. So start there and stick with it. It will be so worth it! You can do this!

Lastly, loving God is also something we *can* do. One way we show Him that is by doing our best to live His commandments (see John 14:15). And by the way, when we say we are "keeping His commandments," that doesn't mean we are perfectly and completely doing every single thing He has ever asked us to do. I believe, though, that it *does* mean we won't weigh out whether or not we want to do something the Lord has asked of us, and deliberately decide to break that particular commandment just because we really want to.

Other ways we can show our love for God include being kind, loving, and helpful to others, and learning about Him through the things He's given us to do that, like the scriptures and the testimonies and counsel of living prophets. We also show Him by telling Him we love Him when we pray, and by spending time with Him as we pray. The thing is, when we do any of these things, He blesses us and usually makes us *feel* good to let us know we're *doing* good. And it helps us want to do good even more.

So does all this sound hard? It really isn't. Truthfully, though, sometimes some things about our lives *will* be hard, because that's just part of the process. Something our Father in Heaven wants us to learn is that regardless of how things look, we can still trust Him—trust that He knows what He's doing with our lives, and that He knows how we need to grow to become who we're meant to be. We need to come to the point where we have so much faith in Him, that we will always choose Him, so matter what. So if something really hard happens in our lives, will we still love God and choose Him, or not? Will we still love Him even if—well, even if *anything?* What He wants is for us to give Him our hearts. He'll still want them even if they're broken, you know. Actually, *especially* if they're broken. But the good thing is, He'll fix them for us, too—and not because we'll be mad at Him if He doesn't do it quick enough, or if it looks like He might not do it at all, but because we'll love Him forever, whether He does it or not, and come what may. Oh, but don't worry. He *will* eventually heal your heart. That's one of His specialties!

But those three little steps back there to becoming perfect in Christ? They really aren't that hard, especially not with everything we receive in exchange. The most marvelous thing of all is that after you've done that for a while, heaven itself is going to tell you that you're doing a great job, and that you are loved. And then you're probably going to look around at everything you didn't get done, or could have done, or at least maybe *should* have done and say, "Is this being addressed to *me*? How could it be? I'm trying, but in my opinion, I just barely get by. I'm nowhere *near* good enough!"

Yet, somehow, through the beautiful plan of happiness, if you've come to the Savior and repented and given Him your heart, if you love your Heavenly Father and love and bless His children, and if you are pure in heart because you have denied yourself all ungodliness, you really and truly are good enough for "his grace [to be] sufficient for you, that by his grace ye may be perfect in Christ" (Moroni 10:32).

Suddenly, you will actually *feel* good enough (in a humble sort of way, of course), because in a bigger way than anything that's ever happened to you before, you will know and *feel* how loved you are. That will make you want to treat everyone else the way this incredible love inside you makes you feel. That's what charity is. It's the love Heavenly Father gives to all those who are true followers of His Son (see Moroni 7:48). And once you feel that tremendous, incredible love from Him, then you have it inside you to give to others. Plus, you will know how, and you will want to.

Then you just stick with it. As you do, you'll find that living the gospel and loving people is much easier than it used to be. You'll have changed so much that you'll be more like Christ, because that's just what being His faithful follower does to a person. Plus, you'll have the companionship of the Holy Ghost—that incredible feeling of warmth and comfort—on an ongoing basis. That will be your reward for sticking with it. Of course, there will always be things to deal with of one kind or another. That's life. But knowing how loved you are, and having the Holy Ghost with you makes life very sweet. It is worth it! And it is something we actually CAN do (unlike all that overwhelming, depressing, unrealistic stuff we sometimes *think* we have to do). So, let's all do this! Let's all come unto Christ, and have all this good stuff happen to us. What a great plan!

Okay, about the rest of this book now. It's basically a book for those of us who aren't (never-were, never-gonna-be) perfect little girls-in-whirls, but are just everyday Latter-day Saint women, doing the best we can in life. It has a little bit of this and that on a variety of subjects, events, or situations that come up in life. It's pretty random, kind of like life is.

One thing I've noticed about life is that even if something happens that was sort of disastrous at the time, it will make a great story to tell later on! So, some of these random and unrelated poems here are my "stories" of one kind or another. And some of them are what I've learned about how wonderful the gospel of Jesus Christ truly is. My hope is that you'll feel that when you read those.

By the way, the rest of the things in this book are thoughts or observations that my brain decided to compose about something or the other when I wasn't looking, because it was bored. In order to keep my brain happy, I write them down. I figure that a happy brain is . . . uh . . . a happy brain! That's gotta be a good thing, right?

Anyway, I hope you enjoy these and can relate to some of what's here, and maybe you will think of some of your own stories that you can share with the sisters you know. Opening our hearts to each other about who we really are and how life honestly is, helps each of us feel more like we're all in this together. Because we are, you know.

XO,
Victoria

Don't Keep the Change

(Sometimes women get married with a list of things they hope to change about their husbands. But when men get married, they usually hope their wives will *never* change!)

My gosh! My heck!
My dream-come-true
Has just proposed to me!
And he's about as perfect
As a guy could ever be!

I really can't believe it—
He's handsome and he's smart;
He's funny, but still sensitive,
With such a giving heart.

And when he holds me in his arms,
I absolutely melt!
I feel a feeling far more fond
Than former feelings felt.

He's so extremely spiritual.
I love his testimony!
He's absolutely genuine—
Not insincere or phony.

He's good with kids and I just know
He'll be a perfect dad.

He's very strong but gentle.
Why, I've never seen him mad!

He's super fun to be with,
But he's so hardworking too—
Responsible about the things
A real man needs to do.

He lives up to his priesthood too,
In everything he does.
He's just about as good as any man
There ever was.

He fits the list I wrote in Laurels
Right down to the letter.
And once we wed I'll change him
Into someone even better!

Just for the record, my husband is great and does not need me to change him! The inspiration for this poem came from my friend Merrilee Boyack's book *Strangling Your Husband Is Not an Option: A Practical Guide to Dramatically Improving Your Marriage.* One of the chapters is titled "But How Do I Change My Husband?" and the next chapter is called "No, Really, How Can I Change Him?"

The point here, however, is that focusing our desires and efforts in our marriages on changing our husbands, isn't exactly the most bonding, wise, or effective thing we can do for our marriages. For starters, it really doesn't work. It also changes us from our husbands' sweethearts into their *mothers*. Not a good thing.

Brushing Up on the Basics

You know I love you madly,
And I'm thrilled to be your wife.
I promised I'd share *all* with you—
My heart, my soul, my life,

My hugs and all my kisses,
And the rest of all me, too.
Yes, everything I'll have or be
I vowed to share with you.

Although I meant it, darling,
Can I make one small thing clear?
I said that I'd share everything—
But NOT my toothbrush, dear!

Ha! No, this doesn't really happen, thank goodness. I absolutely ADORE my husband, Jay. He is so wonderful and amazing, and I would always want to do whatever I could for him. But no, I wouldn't like it if he used my toothbrush (not that he's ever asked!).

O, Tell a Tale o' JELL-O

Marlo Mormarello,
Hair of halo yellow,
Grates some carrot peel-o
For her family's JELL-O.

Pineapple then follows,
Topped with mini-mellows.
Many moms tell Marlo
This makes swell-o JELL-Os.

"Fussy little fellows
Happily will swallow
Carrots in the JELL-O,"
Friends in Provo tell-o.

So Marlo molds the JELL-O,
Then naps below their willow.
But soon she hears a bellow,
And pops up from her pillow.

Woeful hubby Rolo,
Sighs, and says with sorrow,
"Is this carrot JELL-O
For *dessert* tomorrow?"

Marlo goes to Rolo,
And hugs her frowning fellow.

"Sweetie, please be mellow.
This is *healthy* JELL-O!

Kiddos watch you, dear-o.
Eat it, and they'll follow.
You will be my hero
When our trio's tall-o."

For his darling Marlo,
He would drink Tabasco.
If she's pleased by carrot JELL-O,
He is glad she'd ask-o.

So Rolo ate with gusto.
The kids grew up perfecto.
"That JELL-O's been around for flippin' years now,"
He'll reflect-o.

But Marlo's JELL-O hero Rolo
Is a happy fellow,
Since both of them still work on pleasing
One another well-o.

And whether "healthy" JELL-O or
Some other sacrifice,
Marriage lived this way, helps it be hallowed.
And that's nice.

I love the following quote by President James E. Faust: "There are a few simple, relevant questions which each person [in the marriage] . . . should honestly ask in an effort to become 'one flesh.' First, am I able to think of the interest of my marriage and spouse first before I think of my own desires? . . . Our homes should be among the most hallowed of all earthly sanctuaries. In the enriching of marriage the big things are the little things. It is a constant appreciation for each other and a thoughtful demonstration of gratitude" (James E. Faust, "Enriching Your Marriage," *Ensign,* Apr. 2007, 4–8).

It *is* nice when both the husband and wife conduct their marriage this way. I realize that I'm one incredibly blessed woman since that's what Jay and I try to do. I also realize though, sisters, that this isn't always the current reality for many of us. Perhaps it can still be a "star to steer by"—something to gradually work toward while considering some of the little things that President Faust talks about. However, regardless of our circumstances, we can always decide to do what we *can* do. And what we can do in any given situation might be completely different from what someone else may be able to do in their circumstances. But I have such a testimony of the fact that the Lord does accept our efforts when we're trying to do what we can, even if it doesn't seem nearly as good as what someone else is doing! President Faust also said, "If you have done your best, which you usually do, your humble offering, whatever it may be, will be accepted and pleasing to the Lord" (James E. Faust, "Instruments in the Hands of God," *Ensign,* Nov. 2005, 115–16).

Also, maybe our earnest efforts won't immediately change some of the things we desire most at the moment. But when we do what is right and good, regardless of the momentary outcome, we can have that sweet assurance in our hearts that we are about our Father's business, which is to live righteously and to love and bless where we can. Our Heavenly Father wants us to have happy marriages and happy homes. And something you can *absolutely count on* is the fact in one way or another, every sacrifice and righteous action you perform will be blessed by Him for your good and the good of others.

That's nice, too! Really trusting in that can help us remember that *no matter what* our individual situations are, we can always strive, even in simple ways, to be faithful followers of the Savior.

Oh, and about the carrot JELL-O there—I've heard Jay make comments so many times about how when he was growing up, he'd go to a ward social and there would be all these JELL-O salads with *carrots* in them, which he thought was the worst thing ever! So since my brain composes these things mostly on its own and then just sort of gives them to me, I guess it decided that it needed to write something about carrot JELL-O!

Personally, making carrot JELL-O sounded like a pretty decent idea to me . . .

Working on Sunday

I must admit that in the past (I'm somewhat sad to say),
That Sunday sometimes felt like not a very peaceful day.

Our family was a big one and at church, we seemed so noisy.
I worried they could probably hear us all the way to Boise.
I wanted us to all be there because the gospel's true.
I knew it and I wanted for our kids to know it, too.

I love the Saints. I love to learn. But often was the week,
I'd hardly hear a word that anyone at church might speak.
I yearned to feel that sweetness when the sacrament was blessed,
And yet, there were those times when I, instead, felt mostly stressed.

A child would talk, a book would fall, the baby then would wail,
A toddler might announce his bathroom needs in loud detail.
A son perhaps was out of sorts. A daughter poked or whined.
Though some were being good, we were distracting, all combined.

I hoped our family wouldn't mar the reverence of the service,
And helping them stay quiet often left me drained and nervous.
I typically felt bad for those who sat a row behind us.
The members, though, were kind and we were told they didn't
mind us.

But I was always doing something. I was in and out.
Up and down. Back and forth. Over and about.
My husband's always wonderful, and worked with all this too.

But there was often more than even both of us could do.

Although our older ones would try to help us with the younger,
Our meetings often left me with a longing sort of hunger.
But we attended weekly, though at times, I wondered why,
On days that made me ask if I should laugh or I should cry.

Why even go if it's like that? And wouldn't it make sense
To be involved in something that felt calmer and less tense?
A peaceful mountain visit might not leave me feeling stressed;
The kids could wander through its beauty—I could simply rest.

But that was not an option since it *was* the Sabbath day.
We'd do our best to keep it in the Lord's appointed way.
And our attending church was something vital we would do,
Although at home, we tried to keep the Sabbath holy too.

And week by week, it made a difference, always being there.
It took some time, but slowly, they began to grow aware
Of how to act when we're in church. And how else would
they know,
Unless we went and showed them by example when we'd go?

They knew it was important since that's where we'd always be.
That's part of why our presence was significant to me.
I went not just because "I should" or due to ceremony.
Instead, our loud attendance was my silent testimony.

This is almost exactly how it was for us for years and years as we worked on helping our kids learn the importance of Sunday worship at church. I remember that during this time, I was asked to give a talk in sacrament meeting on reverence! I figured it was probably like helping the person who could use a better understanding of the principle of tithing or something, by asking them to speak on that subject so they could learn more about how and why they should do it. I made the comment during my talk that I felt like a Boy Scout whose specialty was burned Spaghetti-o's, being asked to give a class in Relief Society on gourmet cooking!

Handle with Kid Gloves

We'd just come home from church on Easter, when my son,
soon four,
Was tugging on my dress the moment we walked through
the door.
"Mommy! Will you *please* go get a glove that I can wear?"
I went and put my keys away, then rested in a chair.
"I have a glove, but what's it for?" That seemed a fair request.
I have to say that what he told me made me quite impressed.
"Sister Hutchins told us that our spirit's like a hand.
A glove is like our body." And he seemed to understand.
"My body moves around because inside it, there's my spirit."
He'd grasped the whole analogy, and I was thrilled to hear it!
I love analogies—don't touch pornography or snakes;
A "little bad" in shows is just like cockroaches in cakes;
Repentance takes out dirt like it was bleach or good detergent . . .

My thoughts were interrupted by a cry that sounded urgent!
"I need the glove right NOW!" Scott begged, and when I asked
him why,
He cried, "If I don't wear a glove, my teacher says, I'LL DIE!"

Awww . . . This is one of those "Funny and/or Adorable Things Our Kids Did" stories we will tell forever, especially because he was so sincere (and so adorable!). Despite Scott's amusing—although distressing to him at the time—conclusion, I was still an impressed mommy for the way he'd remembered most of the basics of then Elder Boyd K. Packer's classic analogy on life, death, and resurrection. I've also thought about how this also makes a great illustration of the way we can sometimes have most of the general facts regarding an issue, but might still come to a conclusion as wildly off-base as the one Scott drew here. Anyway, I love this funny little story and I'm hoping it won't become too embarrassing or annoying to Scott, who is now fifteen.

Hopefully Not Holesome Fun

A trampoline always provides instant fun!
Of all things we've bought, this is better than any.
We've gotten replacements for mats a few times,
But still, on the whole, it's been worth every penny.
Whenever the kids have their friends here, they're on it;
It's something that just about everyone likes.

(One hint from experience: have them be careful
That nobody jumps on it wearing their spikes . . .)

Unbelievably, this actually happened! I laughed so hard at Bill Cosby's line where he was talking to one of his sons and said something like, "Well, let me ask you this, son. Did you have your BRAIN with you at the time?" Some things just make you wonder a little, don't they?

A Tragic, Movieing Tale

Oh, belov-ed DVD,
Who hath put a scratch on thee?
Henceforth, it won't be too groovy,
Trying to watch a grooved-up movie.
Please think not my deed too brash,
If I fling thee in the trash.

Is there anyone with kids who hasn't had to do this? If so, I nominate you Queen of the Mommies, because your children must be practically perfect, and you deserve it!

I'm Flush with Advice

Don't ever let a toy get in the toilet.
A tiny one can still be a destroylette.
A toy let in the toilet
From a darling girl or boylet,
Can cause plumbing problems
You will *not* enjoylet.

My sweet husband, who loathes plumbing, has probably had to deal with more "toilet toys" of one kind or another than just about any daddy on the planet! He can personally vouch for the havoc and trauma brought about by random objects that mysteriously find their way into the toilet.

Untierful

I'm making a beautiful cake with four tiers,
The most *elegant* thing I've attempted in years.

The icing is made and the layers are cooling.
My three-year-old's watching intently and drooling.

I go change the laundry from washer to dryer,
Then print out a Young Women's fireside flyer.

I do a few calls that I needed to make,
Then I'm back to my four-tiered and fabulous cake.

I first see the crumbs and the mess by the chair,
Then notice his smeared, happy face over there.

I've also seen moments too quickly make years.
We finish our three-tiered and fabulous cake
With no tears.

This is actually just sort of a fantasy. Well, not the part about dealing with kids eating some cake they weren't supposed to, or how learning to look at the big picture in situations can help us deal with things in a calmer and more loving way. That happened! But the cake decorating part? Pure fantasy. I don't really do any cake "decorating" much more significant than shaking some of those little chocolate sprinkles onto the top of a frosted cake, or maybe putting a piped edge or doodad on a pie, cookie, or cake. I'm a big admirer, though, of those with a talent for cake decorating.

But even if I don't decorate cakes, I do have a great frosting recipe I'll share with you. I saw it years ago in a magazine, and I've used it ever since. It's super simple, not overly sweet, and is so yummy that everyone who hasn't tried it before will want to know how you made it. I always give the recipe to anyone who asks for it. (If you're someone people expect a fabulous and extravagant recipe from, I guess you could just let them assume you did a variation on some amazing, complicated mousse recipe in order to make it.)

A little note about this recipe: If you frost a layer cake with this frosting, and you're taking it somewhere in the car with an eleven-year-old holding it, BE CAREFUL! The top layer *will* slide right off onto the floor of the car, and then you'll have to go back home and try to figure out a way to still use the one layer you have left. Plus you'll have to take your dog out to the car to eat all the cake off the floor for you. Actually, even if you're not in a car, do be careful with a layer cake frosted with this delicious frosting because it's slippery between layers.

Fabulous Mousse Frosting

1 small (8 oz.) container Cool Whip, thawed *(you can use the sugar-free version)*
1 small (3.5 oz.) package instant pudding *(sugar-free is okay)*
¾ to 1 cup milk *(experiment to see which amount you like best)*

Mix the pudding and milk until smooth, then gently fold in Cool Whip. Use right away or refrigerate. Try different flavors for different uses. Chocolate or vanilla puddings make delicious frostings. Add 1 tsp. of vanilla, almond, or coconut extract to the vanilla. Lemon or cheesecake puddings make fantastic fruit dips.

A Short Lesson about Snakes as Pets

Something we've learned about snakes without doubt—
Despite how they're caged,
They'll someday get out.

Yep. We've had LOTS of snakes. Some of them for not very long either, because they *do* get out. This is especially true if you have a lot of kids who have lots of friends, and they all want to hold the snake! Our most notorious cage-getter-outer was a very nice, four-and-a-half foot gopher snake named Cuddles. Well, he was also named Slither. Slither is the name he came with, but some of us thought he should be called Cuddles instead. We never really could agree on what he should be named, so it ended up that the name he was called, depended on who was holding him. Anyway, I won't go into all the reasons and ways he was able to get out, but let's just say he was very good at it. The only thing is, he didn't know what to do *after* he got out. He'd go to all the effort and maneuvering to get out of his cage, and then go hide in a dresser drawer. Usually the same dresser drawer.

There was one time I can think of when he tried something different, but it didn't really work out too well for him. Unfortunately, for some reason he decided that our daughter Amber's bed would be a good place to hide. She's a fairly sound sleeper, but when he crawled across her face, she screamed, then grabbed him and plastered him against the wall. The poor thing stayed where he had slid down the wall and under the bed, until we came to put him back safely in his cage and away from Amber. Come to think of it, this could have been the very reason why he was never willing to try anything more daring than slipping into a dresser drawer. He might not have escaped very far, but at least he was safe! There are some people whom you just don't want to wake up suddenly, or until they're ready to get up. I learned that pretty quickly from some of my own personal encounters with a sleeping Amber!

Maybe he finally figured out a little bit better way to escape, though, because one time he was really gone—for a year! We thought he had gotten away for good that time and had joined all his little snakey friends, wherever it is that snakes go when they escape in a Southern California neighborhood—maybe to other people's dresser drawers! After all, we had checked all *our* dresser drawers, and there was no sign of Cudther (or Slithles—I thought maybe for brevity's sake here, I might try a combo name instead of saying Cuddles/Slither every time. Guess it doesn't really work very well though, does it). Anyway, first we thought the snake was just somewhere in the house, but we never saw any indication of that. Still, one of our friends refused to come inside our house for a very long time. Finally, after enough time had gone by, we all basically decided he was gone forever. But of course, he wasn't. He was just hiding very, very well this time. Then one of our friends eventually found him. Fortunately, it wasn't the friend who was absolutely terrified of snakes. But, yeah, the friend who found him *did* scream.

("Oops, sorry. We, uh, didn't really know that snake was still around. He's actually very sweet. Please don't scream. I'm getting him. Okay, here we go. I'll just . . . Oh no, I forgot! We don't have his cage anymore. Uh, well, why don't you, um, wait right here while I take him and go, uh . . . um . . . Oh! While I go put him *in a drawer!*")

Adorable Little Hamsters

Here's a small fact about hamsters that's true:
They get out too.

Yep, again. You know, I have soooooo many snake stories! I could probably write an entire book called *Snake Stories,* all about the crazy snake adventures that took place at our house over the years. (The Bradford stories are the best, but they will have to wait for another time.) With hamsters, on the other hand, the story is very simple and always the same. The book, which I would call *Hamster Stories,* would go like this:

> *Once upon a time, there were some hamsters who lived at these people's house. One by one, many of them got set down somewhere by the person holding them, for only a minute. When the person came back to get their hamster, they went right to where it was supposed to be. And they were very sad, because for some reason, the hamster wasn't there anymore, even though they were sure this was right where they had put it.*
>
> *Then some other hamsters would get out of the cage from time to time, because hamsters do that a lot too. But it doesn't matter why a hamster was out, because the rest of the story is always exactly the same for all the hamsters, and it goes like this:*
>
> *Then the hamster went and lived in the people's couch.*
>
> THE END

Okay, to be honest, we've only had one hamster that we think lived in our couch for a short time. But all the other hamsters wanted to. Just like Sliddles (or Cuther—I thought I'd try again on the name combining thing . . . I think I was trying to combine too equally before. I like it much better this time. As a matter of fact, I really do like both of these names! Too bad I never thought of them sooner). So, just like how Sliddles always hid in a drawer—if I refer to the snake again, I'll call him Cuther, just to be fair, to whom or what I'm not sure. But if there's one thing I've learned from having kids, it's that having everything be FAIR is the most important thing in the universe! Anyway, so just like how Cuther always hid in a drawer, a hamster always goes to the couch to hide. I don't have to give "the hamster" here a name though, since *every* hamster always goes to the couch because they all want to crawl up inside it and make a little house. But since you already know they're going to do that, they're not all that hard to catch. And the nice thing is, if someone other than you happens to see the hamster before you do, they don't usually scream.

Those Other St.'s

It's hard to have a St. Bernard.
A doggy St., he ain't . . .
But not a terror either
As a very general rule.

He's loving and he's smart—
I'd keep his mind and heart,
But if I had the wherewithal
To oust another part,
I'd rid him of his
Quite unsaintly
Drool.

Anyone who's ever been to our house knows we have a St. Bernard. His name is Barney, which was his name when we got him. But "Barney" didn't seem to me to be the best name for a dog, since almost every kid in the world knows the other Barney. (If you don't, go find a couple of children and ask them who Barney is. That will prove my point. Wait, I can prove it even better. Get online, go to Google, and type in "Barney." At the time of this writing, 23,700,000 sites come up. Not every single one of them is about Barney the purple dinosaur, but *almost* all of them are! Really, go see. Then type in "Abraham Lincoln." There are 15,200,000 sites! I realize that Lincoln hasn't been around as recently as Barney, and that he doesn't have a really cool song either, but Barney's place in history isn't quite as important as Lincoln's. I mean, c'mon! Barney's not even real, for goodness sake.)

So, for those millions of good reasons, I didn't think "Barney" was a very good name for a dog. However, Jay thought it was morally wrong to name a dog something other than the name it originally had. I could have made the point that if you went and bought some new and absolutely delicious doggie treat, your dog would very quickly learn the name of that new treat, if every time you went to give him one, you said the name of the treat. (By the way, I just say "him" here because Barney is a "him." I mean no disrespect to the all the dog-ettes out there.) I know for a fact it would take Barney about two days to recognize the name of a Doggie Bacon Yum-Yum, if it really did taste like bacon. (I wouldn't know if it actually does taste like bacon or not, because I just made that name up. Plus I would never try even an infinitesimal crumb of it to see how it tasted, if it was real, even though our friend Larry Watts eats Milk Bones and says they're really good.)

Well, maybe Barney could have learned a new name, but maybe that just isn't a very nice thing to do to a dog. I don't know. Also, Barney was Jay's Christmas present that year, and around here, when it's your pet, you get to name it. Of course, the rest of us are free to suggest the name we think the pet should have.

And then, if it's a pet that belongs to the family, naming could turn into a bit of a circus, like it was with our adorable dog, Olive. When she was a brand-new puppy, many names were suggested, but the list was narrowed down to a final three. Now, I'm going to tell you what those three names were, and you will quite probably think what I would think if someone told them to me. "Those were the three *best* names? What were the *other* names? They must have been *really* bad!" I admit that all three names may seem a little strange for a dog. They were Olive, Brie, and Isis. (We tend to be "creative thinkers" in our family, all right? Still, I'm not sure why there were two food names and one goddess name. I remember that "Olive" was suggested because the puppy was black like olives. Okay, so maybe that's not so creative, but we do allow suggestions from all ages of family members.) It was then decided that the full name, if chosen, would be "Olive Oyl," like Popeye's girlfriend, who also had black hair. (See, at least it's consistent.) The supporters of "Brie" simply passionately loved the name. And I think "Isis" might have been submitted by someone who had heard the name at school when they were studying Egyptian culture, since she is one of their goddesses. (Isis is the goddess of motherhood and fertility, which I figured we were doing fine on. I did *not* vote for "Isis.")

Finally, the family gathered so that everyone could present his or her opinion about why a particular name should be chosen. I don't remember exactly how it all went, but speeches were given, and there were signs that had been made in support of some of the names. There was also a supporting song some of the kids had made up, which was sung so many times that our seventeen-year-old daughter, Jenni, who was five at the time, just sang it for me this morning when I asked her if she remembered when we chose Olive's name. Obviously, the name "Olive" won, for reasons less obvious than it was simply the best name. The three names that made it to the "finals" were about equal, wouldn't you say? (Well, minus the Isis issue. . . .) Anyway, I only bring all this up to point out that pet-naming is kind of a big deal at our house, along with the fact that we all "help" the pet owner out by giving him or her lots and lots of good suggestions and advice about what the pet's name should be.

So, a few days after we got Barney, we were still talking about the name thing a little, when I had to go down to get his dog license. I was filling out the paperwork for it, when I got this great idea! "Barney" was not a good name for a dog. But what about "Bernie"? You know, as in "St. Bernard"? Maybe it's a little contrived, but I still thought it was kind of cute. *Waaaay* better than "Barney." And it wouldn't be confusing to Jay's new dog because "Barney" and "Bernie" sounded so similar. Not similar enough to a human, though, that they would sing the purple dinosaur song every time they heard his name. I honestly thought it was a perfect solution—a clever one, even, and felt a little pleased with myself that I had come up with it. I paid the licensing fee and filled out the paperwork for "Bernie." I was so excited to go home and share the great news of my wonderful idea.

Jay hated it. HATED it! When I asked him why, he said because "Bernie" was a "people name." A people name? How about the fact that "Barney" was both a people name *and* a purple-dinosaur name? Not only that, but our dogs before this had been named Maxwell, Olive, Nichole, Sam, and Frodo. What about those people names? (Well, okay, to be fair, I should explain that Jay didn't give any of those dogs their names. Plus, the last two names on that list are hobbits.)

Although I had thought the idea for a name transition from the dinosaurified "Barney" to a far more neutral "Bernie" was a good one, I believed it was a much better idea for Jay to be happy with his dog's name. After all, it was Jay's dog. If he wanted the big lug's name to be Barney, Barney it would be—that is, except for once each year, when the city of Redlands sends us a letter reminding us that "Bernie" needs his license renewed!

Getting Along Swimmingly

After thinking it out, I've decided
That fish make the very best pets.
Though perhaps that sounds odd,
Fish are fairly unflawed,
And in most ways, as good as it gets.

They never go chew up your couches,
Or chew hundreds of holes in the hose.
They don't *sit* there and beg
And don't claw up your leg,
Like a cat as it climbs up your clothes.

If you buy them the wrong kind of fish food,
They don't *backstroke* away, looking miffed.
What they also don't do
Is leave presents for you,
Like a little dead mouse as a gift.

You *won't* find fish drinking from toilets
Like their personal porcelain dishes.
Plus they're simple to bury.
Skip the pet cemetery!
Just flush, and they sleep with the fishes.

Fish rarely will bother your neighbor
By barking all night until dawn.
They also don't prowl

Through their trash cans, or howl,
And they don't leave a mess on their lawn.

Fish *aren't* really very demanding,
Insisting to go for a walk—
Pleading, "Come get my bowl,
And let's have a nice stroll
While I visit each fish on the block."

Although it's not *that* fun to pet them
(since scale-stroking won't make them purr),
Pet their backs and their tails,
And your clothes *won't* have scales,
Like the hair you'd collect from pets' fur!

And they *won't* make a home in your sofa,
Like hamsters just *love* to go do!
Or like puppies who choose
From among all your shoes,
Fish *won't* gnaw the pair that is new.

Fish don't squawk non-stop like some birds do,
And your home can be *calm* with them in it.
Plus, you won't find one day
That your fish flew away,
When you left their bowl open *one minute.*

They don't *try* to crawl out of their fishbowls
If a lid's not on tight, by mistake.

If a fish *does* get out,
Will your friends shriek and shout?
Prob'ly not. But they *will* with a snake!

Some folks think a *fish*
Is as good of a pet,
As anyone ever could possibly get.

While I'm *glad* that each kid
Got the pets that they did,
I *don't* need more help here with flipping my lid!
One *more* living thing I'm responsible for—
Just *this* one,
Then *that* one,
Then just this *one* more . . .
Regardless of who'll feed or clean or adore it,
Overall, *I'm* still responsible for it,

'Cause *I'm* making sure there aren't pets in the bed,
And I might not *feed* them, but make sure they're fed.
Pets got away? I help *find* where they fled.
Fix or replace what they chew on or shred,
Help follow through on the things the vet said,
Specify who cleans up trash that they spread,
Quickly dispose of the birds they behead,
Deal with the hair that they constantly shed,
If a pet *dies* (something *all* parents dread),
I help decide what to do, now it's dead.

The kids have learned *working* and *love* from a pet,
So *that's* made it worth any headaches or sweat.
Still . . .
Someday, *those* pets will be gone,
then *I'll* wish
For *one* little, peaceful, adorable fish!

Every single word about each and every pet here is the absolute truth. And there's more. So much more! In addition to the pets already mentioned, over the last couple of decades we've had lizards, a pot-bellied pig, frogs, turtles, white rats, eels, a grouse, guinea pigs, and—for a couple of days—a tarantula!

Some Changes in the Organization

There – once – was – a – man – with – an – organized – life.
His – organized – mind – chose – an – organized – wife.
He – drove – in - his – fuel-saving – car – every - day
To – his – well-kept – office – in – a – well-routed – way.

He – left – right -- at – seven, – but – he'd -- never – leave – before
His -- wife – came – and – stood – for – her - kiss – at – the – door.
He – got – to – his – office – just – at – 7:22,
And – did – all – the – work – that – the – organized – do.

He – traveled – back– home, – hung – his – keys – on – a – hook,
He – dined – with – his – wife, – brushed – his – teeth, – read –
 a – book.
He – listened – to – Bach – 'til – the – eight – o'clock – chime.
Then — planned – his – tomorrow – so – he – wouldn't –
 waste – time.

His – life – was – just – perfect – with – its – organized – ways.
He – knew – he'd – be – happy – for– the – rest – of – his – days.

Then they had some children and his life forever changed.
His bookshelves and priorities were quickly rearranged.
He soon found forts of blankets in what used to be his den;
Untied his ties from necks of puppies every now and then,

Wiped Slurpees from inside his car and spit-up off his suit,
Drove kids to elementary school before his work commute.

At night, he heard beginning violin screech down the hall;
And though his life was different, here's his comment on it all:

"My former world seemed perfect, but I never understood
How joyful life could be—that less-than-perfect could feel good!
I liked my mind of order and I'm not sure where it went,
But still, I'm very happy and feel perfectly content . . .
(although I wish the hook I hang my keys on wasn't bent,
and the dresser in our bedroom didn't have that scratch and dent,
and I knew where someone put those bills that hadn't yet
been sent,
and there wasn't purple paint out on the patio cement,
and I knew how all that money that I *used* to have gets spent . . .
. . . and I wish I had a bit of time that's free, just like before . . .)

But all those things are small ones,
My sweet "little ones" mean more.

He went and hugged his children and the wife he'd have forever,
So glad they shared this "less-than-perfect" lifetime altogether.

Then once the kids had all left home because they'd finally grown,
And each of them was starting on a family of their own,
He'd walk his perfect, ordered house without a smudge or dent,
Then daydream by that spot of purpled patio cement.

Although I was never the "organized wife" it talks about here, Jay is definitely the model for the "organized man" in this one. Ha! Life with lots of kids, especially when they're little, is quite a shock to the system of an organized type! It wasn't a big surprise to me that this is one of Jay's favorite poems in this collection, and he gets a little misty-eyed when he reads it.

Someone Needs to Hallo-wean

There are mountains of candy left over this year,
'Cuz more trick-or-treaters are typically here.
The kids all have plenty and *I* shouldn't eat it.
Perhaps I should save it 'til sometime we need it.

I'll put it where no one could possibly climb,
Up high on a top closet shelf.
Then one after one accursed piece at a time,
I'll eat the whole thing by myself.

(You think this didn't happen?? Guess again . . . It did!)

At our house, Halloween is usually lots of fun. I can't stand the gruesome or ghoulish stuff, but I love the rest, especially dressing up in whatever costumes we come up with. Most of us in the family enjoy dressing up, and I probably have eight large bins of Halloween costumes, stacked up out in the garage. I typically like to dress up as something different or maybe even a little strange. I guess it's just so me. When I was growing up, I would always roll my eyes at the girls who had to be something "cute," with ponytails or fairy wings or pom-poms or tiaras. I wanted to be something *interesting* or maybe just a weird-looking person. And I still do, I guess. When I was first married, I spent most of the day getting ready for a ward Halloween party. I loved my costume. I was a Martian, and I had painted myself green. I had antennas, and my hair was twisted up everywhere. I looked great! But when my husband got home, he was horrified.

"I thought you'd probably be all made up like a princess or something." Oops! Wrong fairytale.

Some of our kids like to get really dressed up too. Our daughter Christa would win first place every year at her work's Halloween party. Her last year there, she made herself into an old woman, and her costume and mannerisms were so authentic all day long, that some of the people there didn't even know who she was or why she was there all day! Amber, who is a few years younger (and on a mission right now), likes to go all-out in dressing up too, and also goes all-out in turning any simple event she's involved with into something exciting and fun. Both Christa and Amber told me that when people asked them how they came up with ideas like that, they each said, "Oh, you'd just have to meet my mom, then you'd understand." (Hmm . . . I'm still trying to figure that comment out. Is it sort of a compliment, or is it a disclaimer?)

Oh, then there's the Halloween candy! The kids have always been nice to me, and they usually let me have most of their Almond Joys. Mmm. Three of my most favorite things—nuts, chocolate, and coconut—all in one place at the same time. Then when it comes to their own candy, we have some kids who would be so happy when they came home with a bunch of candy. Although we have treats here, and candy sometimes, it's not something we have every day at our house. Then we have some kids who loved going trick or treating, but didn't particularly care for candy. After coming home from the ward's Trunk or Treat, they'd pick out a few pieces to eat, and would let the rest of the kids have whatever they wanted of what was left.

Our daughter Melissa would usually get tons of candy at Halloween, because she'd hit the surrounding neighborhoods after the Trunk or Treat. She would take her haul of candy, organize and categorize it, and have it all ready for Candy Store, which the kids would typically play the day after Halloween. Whoever wanted to would set up a candy store in their bedroom. Then when everyone was ready, they would be invited to visit each other's candy stores, where they could bargain and trade for the candies they liked best. After Candy Store was over, Melissa would put her remaining candy away in a little layered chest, separated by type and category. Although she might eat a piece every once in a while, she liked the way it *looked* more than she liked eating it. When Halloween came around the next year, she still had candy left, which she would then throw away because it was officially one year old.

In the meantime though, Melissa made good use of her beautiful treasure chest of candy. You'd be amazed at what a brother or sister would be willing to do for their favorite piece of candy at the right moment! Sibs (short for siblings, and what some of our kids prefer to call their brothers and sisters, as in, "My sibs and I were just about to jump off the roof onto the trampoline when . . .") might go upstairs or out to the car to get something Melissa needed, bring her a drink of water, participate in some activity with her that might be her favorite but not theirs, do one of her chores, and more, only limited by Melissa's ability to come up with new uses for the power and appeal of her carefully stockpiled candy.

Incidentally, although we required the kids to do certain chores themselves, many other things were available for cooperative negotiation, such as offering someone enough of the right kind of candy. We would intervene if we felt something was inappropriate for whatever reason, but did allow occurrences that we felt were unwise, if they were done by someone who was old enough to make sound decisions. For example, one of our teenagers once paid Jared, who was probably ten at the time, $37.00 to clean up the doggie-doo in the backyard! He was thrilled and very happy to do the job! Usually the "deals" made were more within the norm. And I have to say that Melissa's Halloween candy negotiating was generally pretty reasonable. She's at BYU now, and I've missed her. I could always count on her for a good deal on a Reese's Peanut Butter Cup or maybe even an Almond Joy.

De-liver Me, Please!

"You ought to make him eat those peas!" the other mother cried.
I looked him over doubtfully, while trying to decide—
Should I be encouraging, or should I just insist
He eat each bite of some unwanted food he might resist?

I'd read what's written in the books, but how was *I* to know
When even "experts" disagreed how things like this should go?
These parenting decisions had begun to make me wonder
If I might somehow wreck my kids with some disastrous blunder.

Regarding food, some images from childhood made me shiver,
Remembering the way it was on nights when we had liver.

We absolutely *had* to eat it, and I simply couldn't.
I wasn't being difficult. It's not just that I *wouldn't.*
The flavor made me start to gag whenever I would chew it.
I tried to swallow bites still whole, but it was hard to do it.

Despite my desperate pleading and regardless of my tears,
We still ate "healthy" liver once a month for many years.
My childish mind devised a plan to make the whole thing bearable
Which made those awful liver nights a little bit less terrible.

I'd quickly drink my milk and then I'd cut the liver up.
I'd put each piece into my mouth, then drop it in my cup.
I'd act like I was drinking, and I never did get caught.
(And please don't think I'm proud of this, because I'm really not.)

But such a vivid recollection caused my hesitation.
I wished for pleasant meals instead of tearful child frustration.
So right or wrong, I'd ask the kids at least to try a sliver.
And prayed my choices wouldn't cause them lives with cups of liver.

This is *exactly* what I did while I was growing up, when we had liver for dinner. Once I had kids, it did make me wonder about the best way to handle food issues that came up.

The last line in this poem refers to all the decisions that parents need to make about their children when they really aren't sure what the right answers are. The "lives with cups of liver" ending is a metaphor for the "distasteful results" parents' well-meaning choices might potentially bring into their children's lives.

Most parents yearn to make their children's lives wonderful. As a new parent, doesn't it feel so intimidating that you're responsible for so many decisions in so many areas that could have a lifelong impact on your children? And if you didn't grow up in a gospel home, it can be especially daunting trying to sort them all out. Thank goodness for Relief Society, and for counsel in General Conference, and for wonderful examples all around us. Most of all, thank goodness for a kind Heavenly Father who has given us the gift of the Holy Ghost and the gift of prayer.

Neighbor Hoods???

Our neighbors are so awful that we don't know what to do!
Although we can't be certain, still, we think these things are true:
They break into our home, and then spill syrup on the rug.
They leave the milk out constantly, and break a favorite mug.

They borrow several tools that we find later on the lawn,
Put empty boxes in the cupboard when the cereal's gone.
Then lots of things just disappear—we don't know where
they went.
And, unexplained, possessions end up dirty, cracked, or bent.

They leave the birdcage open, and the back gate open too,
And leave the lids off peanut butter, jelly jars, and glue.

We know we should confront them,
But don't want our friendship wrecked.
Our kids say *they're* not doing this,
Who *else* can we suspect???

It is so true that especially in a big family, you somehow end up with things happening that "nobody" did. I don't know if it's because someone isn't brave enough to tell the truth or it's easier to just say nothing, or because in the ruckus of it all, the person really doesn't realize that he or she is the one who actually did it!

Helping kids learn to tell the truth when it's hard is something we all probably hope to be able to instill in our children, but that's easier said than done. John, our oldest son, was always amazingly truthful when he was growing up. That hasn't been the case with all of our kids, though, so they've probably had John's example explained to them a few thousand more times than they were interested in hearing. But the overall point we make with it is this:

Honesty equals trust, which equals more FREEDOM to have FUN with your FRIENDS.

This little gold nugget of wisdom was shared with us by one of our favorite mentors, the incredibly wonderful Dr. John Lund, when we were about a third of the way through raising our family. Wish we'd heard it sooner! He explains that although being an individual of honesty and integrity is one of the most important building blocks of character, teenagers may not care as much about their emerging characters "in the moment" as they do about being able to have fun with their friends. Including items that are major motivators for our kids in our discussions on honesty will help give them an immediate day-to-day reason to want to have characters of honesty. (See John L. Lund, *How to Hug a Teenage Porcupine*, set of 4 audio CDs [American Fork, Utah: Covenant Communications, 2004]).

For example, the other day, I was taking Scott and his friend Adrian home from high school. Although Scott is good about taking care of his schoolwork and related assignments all on his own, I happened to ask him if he was keeping up on everything in all his classes. When he answered something like, "Basically . . . ," I asked a couple more questions and learned that he had missed two or three assignments in one of his classes. My standard little script, talking about how "if you always attend school, turn in every single assignment, and do a quality job, you will get good grades," was already running in my head as I asked him if it was because he didn't understand the work and needed help with the assignments. There was a pause, and then Scott answered, "No, I already knew everything they were talking about, so I just didn't feel like doing the assignments." Rather than launch into any number of potential mommy lectures and possible discussions of consequences and so on, I thankfully had the wherewithal to take a step back, and realize that I had a golden opportunity before me to reinforce the principle of honesty. I responded to him by laughing and saying, "Well, Scott, parents like to know that their kids are doing all their homework because it's important. But at least you're honest about it! And always being honest, no matter what, is the thing that's going to make us be able to trust you enough to give you the freedom to go do lots of fun things with your friends." I figured that the homework issue itself could be addressed in other ways at another time, but that this chance was too good to pass up.

There was silence for few moments, and then Adrian burst out laughing and said, "Wow, that's the last thing I expected. I was waiting for Scott to get killed or something!"

"Well, yeah. But, I decided it would probably be better to do away with him later, when you weren't around to be a witness, you know?"

Stop Signs

You know that a movie is over
When the credits appear on the screen,
And Christmas is going to come quick
If you've already hit Halloween.

You know that a candle and ketchup
Are just about gone when they sputter.
And closets have *got* to be cleaned
When you can't shut the door for the clutter.

For those who have homes that are blessed
With a teenager son or a daughter,
You know that their shower will stop
Once they've used every drop of hot water.

[We have SO lived this one!]

Clothestraphobia

Just great. I'm afraid something's missing again.
My daughter had worn it, but I'm not sure when.
I love all the girls that we've had in our house,
And over the years, have lent shoes or a blouse.
But each of them finally grew taller than me,
Except for the youngest (we'll still have to see.)

It's sad just how quickly a little one grows,
But I'm glad once they *finally* grow out of my clothes!

[And we've lived this, especially with the *shoes*.]

Regrettefully Yours

(poem for a car-loving son)

I've loved each Corvette
That I've ever mette.
That sleek silhouette's
Still the greatest thing yette.

I don't think I'll gette one—
I don't want the debtte.
If you give me yours, will I take it?
You bette!

It's been fascinating to see the kinds of things our kids have liked, even though we've raised them "all the same" in many respects. Everyone had access to both dolls and Hot Wheels, and no one was ever encouraged or discouraged to play with either one. Everyone took a turn with dishes, we all worked in the yard, and so on. Yet all the boys loved talking about cars, and none of the girls ever did. That's not to say nothing ever crossed the line of stereotypical girl or boy interests. One son, Eric, who has always loved to cook, made a gorgeous lemon meringue pie from scratch all by himself when he was eleven! And of the only three children who like to sew—which I love to do, although I don't do it as much as I used to—two are girls, and other one is a boy. He came to me and asked if I'd teach him how to sew because it looked cool! He's a man now, with a beautiful little family. And he still likes to sew.

Sighcle . . .

It doesn't seem too safe to me to ride a motorcycle.
There's danger from the slightest bump. The risk seems pretty
high-cle.
They speed through traffic unprotectedly. I wonder why-cle.

We *don't* want our kids getting one, or riding loaner-cycles.
(The nurses in the transplant unit call them *"donor-cycles"!*)

I'm sorry. I realize that lots of people just love motorcycles. But I can't get past seeing them on the freeways, looking so exposed and vulnerable. It hit home this year when Nick, in college and riding a motorcycle because it's economical, had a near-miss when a car turned into his lane without seeing him. He avoided the collision by laying the bike down, and he skidded fifteen to twenty feet on his leg. Ow! Fortunately, he got away with "just" terrible road rash, which laid him up for about a week because he hurt too much to move.

The mommy in me was dying to say, "However, if you'd been in a CAR, then probably nothing bad would have . . . blah, blah, blah . . ." But I didn't because he no doubt already *knew* that. It's hard though, sometimes, to not treat our adult children like they're still little kids!

By the way, my friend Pat, who's a surgical nurse, passed along that donor-cycle comment.

Shoet!

Help! I'm in *two* different shoes!
Yes, it's one of those awful-but-true's.
I was trying them on to see which one looked right,
So, one of them's brown and the other's off-white.
My mind got distracted, and now my sad plight,
Is I'm wearing these *two* different shoes!

Oh, help! I'm in *two* different shoes,
And I'm stressed by the what-should-I-do's.
Should I take them both off, wearing no shoes at all?
Find out if there's someone at home I can call?
Appear not to care—just go in and walk tall?
Oh help! I'm in *two* different shoes!

My two different shoes were okay,
Even though I was teaching today.
Announcing our topic, I asked them to try
To think how these two different shoes might apply
To our lesson, and someone told *perfectly* why
I'd be wearing those *two* different shoes!

Ha ha ha! Yep, I've done this a couple of times, but I never ended up talking about it in a class. I remember that one of the times, I was trying on shoes to see which one looked the best with the outfit I was wearing to church, when I got interrupted by one of the kids. I ended up going downstairs to take care of some dire something or other, and once that was done, it was time to leave for church. I grabbed my things and went right out to the car. I didn't even notice that my shoes weren't matching until I got inside the church. The thing is, they didn't just "not match." They weren't even close! I looked down and saw that I was wearing one close-toed black shoe, and one beige sandal. I ended up sitting in the back of the cultural hall during sacrament meeting, and then just took the shoes off and carried them around with me for the rest of the meetings. If people asked why I wasn't wearing any shoes, I just showed them my shoes and we had a laugh over it. It was sort of embarrassing, but I've had worse. None that I'm going to tell here, though!

While Jay and I were talking about this and other embarrassing things, he reminded me of something hilarious that happened to him. When our daughters Amber and Melissa were ages eight and six, they asked Jay if they could paint his toenails. He tends to be a bit of a pushover when it comes to questions asked by little girls, and he had previously let some of his daughters curl his hair, put makeup on him, dress him up for church on Father's Day in sparkly homemade ties, and try out different pairs of earrings on him. So just getting his toenails painted was no big deal. He told the girls that was fine, and then stretched out on the living room floor with his shoes off to wait for Amber and Melissa to go get their supplies. A few minutes later, he was sound asleep. (Although Jay was a fairly light sleeper when we first got married, having a houseful of kids cured that pretty easily! I think a bulldozer could crash through our bedroom wall—if it somehow managed to get up to the second floor, that is—and Jay would peacefully sleep right on through it.) Sometime quite a while later, Jay woke up, stood, and stepped into a pair of flip-flops, which Southern Californians tend to live in during summer—and the rest of the year—and then headed for the grocery store. He'd been in the store for about fifteen or twenty minutes and had a big cart full of groceries, when he happened to look down and saw his feet. The girls had done a lovely job on his toenails! All ten of them (and a little of the surrounding skin of his toes) were beautifully painted a gorgeous shade of bright, hot pink. Oh. He'd forgotten about the toenails. Cringing in embarrassment, Jay immediately took off for the checkout counters. It was a Saturday night and the store was packed. He had to wait in a long line, and it seemed like forever before he was able to dash out to the car where no one would be able to admire his daughters' handiwork. Since we almost always see ward members at the store when we're shopping at that time on a Saturday, I asked Jay if anyone from the ward had seen his toenails. He told me that he didn't know because he'd just kept his head down as low as he could the entire time he was there so that he didn't have to make eye contact with anyone! This is such a great story. And it reminds me about how much I love April Fool's Day because it would be *so* fun to do this sometime to one of the males around here.

Washed Up

While I'm *not* always caught up on laundry,
It goes fairly well, but I *can't* say
I love it.
I remember those days not too fondly,
There was *so* much, I called it my "year's supply"
Of it.

Laundry for *twelve people* on top of everything else that needed to be done . . . Even if older kids did some of their own laundry, do I even need to say how true this one is?

Microwave Cooking's a Blast!

Here's some good info for microwave cooking
We've learned as we've cooked in that mode—

Those toppings for ice cream with lids left on tight,
And eggs put in raw,
Both explode!

Yes, we've had both the egg and the chocolate topping explode. So did everyone else just magically already know all this or something?

Money Lost

Once I found a bag of money so immensely BIG,
I simply couldn't move it. Couldn't *nudge* it!
So, then I tried with all my might,
And you would see it here tonight,
But sadly, I just couldn't seem to *budg-et.*

Just in case you were worried, the bag of money mentioned above ended up as unclaimed property, which a finder is legally allowed to keep after attempts are made to locate its rightful owner. I didn't want you fretting or losing any sleep over someone trying to take money that wasn't his or hers. For your information, NO ONE in my poems ever does that! And if they ever even *tried* to, they'd just have to find themselves *another* poem to be in, because we don't allow that around here!

The Best Christmas Present My Husband Ever Bought Me

I love my GPS!
I now get lost MUCH less!

"Less" is the key word here. Please don't ask me to explain how it is still possible to get lost even with a GPS. It just is. But not as badly.

Exercism

I really want to get in shape—
Get fit and lose some weight.
I'm starting any second now!
It's going to be great!

I'll walk the dog, I'll start to jog,
Or maybe join a gym.
I'll find a fun aerobics class,
Or take a daily swim.

I'll eat less fat and junky stuff,
And strictly start to diet,
Drink water, eat more vegetables—
I'm really going to try it!

I'll buy some weights to lift each day,
And do some great routines.
With yoga or with tennis,
I'll fit back into those jeans!

Though I'm big-boned, I'll look so toned
And ever-so-much thinner.
Let's celebrate the me-to-be
By going out to dinner!

I was asked to write something about exercise for a Relief Society event. This poem happened to come to me very quickly, and I really liked it. I adored the title, which I thought was hilarious (mostly because *I* wouldn't have thought of it—my brain sort of "gave it" to me when I wasn't thinking about it). JoDy, the Relief Society sister who asked me to write it, didn't care for the title though, and simply called it "Exercise." She is probably the sweetest person ever, and that was completely fine with me, since she is the one I wrote it for so they could use it at Relief Society. However, here, I'm calling it "Exercism"! Maybe that's some kind of little passive-aggressive joke about the *evils of exercise.* I'll have to see if I can ask my brain about that . . .

Removable Dents

I do believe I've had my fill of fillings.
I've had enough to last me for forever,
Of shots in gum to get me numb, of drillings—
The next time I would like that done is *never.*

Barring brushing, flossing, and fluoriding,
Here is something you might find exciting,
Guaranteeing no more fillings ever,
But I'll pass . . .
. . . on teeth that smile brightly, sitting nightly
In a glass.

Even though my dentist is both highly skilled and very kind, I still dislike going to the dentist. But when I do go, I always think how truly blessed I am that we have clean, comfortable dental offices to go to, with good numbing stuff and all that. Years ago, I read the fascinating book *The Century of the Surgeon,* by Jurgen Thorwald, and it forever changed my perspective on the day we live in. I am ever so grateful to be here—NOW—instead of living then!

Mystery Meal

Oh, no, what's for dinner?! Today was so busy
That this is the first time I've thought of it.
I'm hoping I'll find something out in the freezer,
And hope that there's really a lot of it.

The times that I'm good about planning our menus,
Our dinner fare isn't in doubt.
But when I *don't* plan, I might just kick cupboards
Then cook us whatever falls out.

"Hey, Mom! What's for dinner?" a hungry son asks me.
I wink. "It's a secret," I go.
And then comes the part
That they *all* know by heart:
"... SO secret, *I* don't even know!"

So true, so true! Sometimes I'm amazingly wonderful about well planned-out menus and meals, and sometimes, it's exactly what you read there. Especially in the past, part of what made menu planning difficult was trying to come up with meals that most of the family actually liked. It can get pretty discouraging to spend time cooking a nice meal, only to have someone ask, "Do I have to eat this?" It certainly would have been easier if all our children had possessed the fully-adult taste buds that our youngest son, Bradford, was apparently born with. From the time he was able to eat solids, he was begging us for more of all kinds of vegetables, green salads, and even fish, which most of our kids haven't liked for some reason. I used to sometimes cook "kid food" for dinner as well as something only Jay and I would want, but once Brad came along, I'd have to make sure I had enough "adult food" for three. I remember having dinner while holding Brad on my lap, eating his feta-crusted salmon along with Jay and me, while the rest of the kids were enjoying their macaroni and cheese!

Cutting Remarks

I own *forty-two* fine pairs of scissors.
Yes, I really like scissors a lot!
I think you can *never* have too many scissors,
No matter how many you've got.

And I use scissors daily for *something*.
They're the handiest things someone owns.
They're for cutting up rags, and for cutting off tags,
And could even be used to cut scones.

(Well, okay . . . We don't *really* make scones here.
But I *keep* saying I'm going to start.
Though the "when" is obscure, when I do, then for sure,
I'll use scissors to cut them apart.)

I use them for cutting up chicken,
And for cutting the meat for a stew.
But before I do *that,* I will trim off the fat,
Which I always use scissors for, too.

They're handy when wrapping up presents,
And they're great to cut gum off a cat.
They're for mushrooms and bows, and to snip off a rose,
And for patterns, and odd this and that.

While I trim off the edges of piecrusts,
And I use them to try and cut hair,

The *one* thing I *don't* cut, is the one I WOULD, but,
Seems I *can't,* since my scissors *aren't there*!

See, I also have *ten* lovely children,
And each of *them* loves scissors too.
And though each one will swear that they *don't* have a pair,
Mine are gone. Where? I don't have a clue!

And I wish they'd stop taking my scissors.
This is getting depressing to me.
Though they need them, no doubt, if they'd just *cut it out,*
Maybe *I* could keep pair forty-three!

I don't *really* have that many pairs of scissors. However, there was a time when I would habitually pick up an inexpensive pair of scissors any time I was out shopping, just to make sure I would have some.

Gist of the List

Fashion
Art
Handicraft
Energy
Electronics

Maintenance
Accounting
Purchasing
Economics

Literature
Government
Religion
Psychology

Grief Counseling
Community Relations
Biology

Relationships
Consulting
Geriatrics
Recreation

Entertainment
Horticulture

Management
Transportation

Home Design
Nutrition
Cuisine
Education

Medicine
Pediatrics
Law
Organization

This is not a list of courses long enough to make you dizzy.
Look at it as just the gist of what we do at home. We're BUSY!

When you're finally home at night, and ask me, "What'd you do, dear?"
I'll just post this list for you. Perhaps you'll get a clue, dear!

Important notice! I'm laughing as I write these last few lines. It's a JOKE, not something to ever really say.

Time Warped

The "five minutes" more that a woman might need 'til she's ready
to go,
Is the same,
As the time that it takes when a man says there's only just "five
minutes" more
In the game.

My ever-patient husband knows that my "five minutes" will usually be *this* kind of five minutes. But I'm working on it. Really.

Sockcess!

If people do laundry, they'll someday inquire:
Just where is that sock that I threw in the dryer?
It's all such a mystery. It *can't* disappear!
Those socks were a pair and now *that* one's not here.

The mystery's been solved. I'm excited to share
I *finally* discovered what happens in there!
The socks are not *missing* for pairs that you need,
Instead, you've got EXTRAs! In dryers, socks breed!

Well, *something* happens to them . . . And I am SO TIRED of unmatching socks!!!!!!! I'm not even sure that's enough exclamation points!!!!!!!!!!!!!!! Yes, I've probably used every method ever invented to keep them matched up, and there are still unmatching socks. This is often because some people don't fold their socks together before putting them into the laundry so that I can clip, safety-pin, sock-lock, pair-it, sock-sorter, glue gun, braid, staple, or weld them together.

When I would observe frequent repeat "offenders," I would sometimes allow *them* to spend an afternoon matching up socks, so they could experience what a very *LONG* time it took to find each sock's perfect mate—especially compared to the half a second it would have taken to fold them together in the first place.

When there were lots more of us at home than there are now, we would sometimes have what I optimistically and euphemistically called a "sock party." Everyone came at the appointed time—attendance at this "party" was mandatory!—and I'd avalanche a decent-sized mountain of unmatching socks onto the floor in the center of the room. We'd all dig through for socks that matched, and each match was rewarded with one peanut M&M. Granted, it's not a huge reward, but if someone ever really elected to work very hard and very long at the sock party, the potential was there to leave with enough M&Ms to fill a pillowcase. Ah, sock parties . . . Such fond memories of watching everyone match up socks instead of just *me* doing it all!

That was in days past. A while back, I determined that although we no longer had our own Mt. Everest of socks, I had spent more than enough years of my life on matching up socks. So I finally just started tossing all the unmatched socks into a bag with any other unmatched socks. Now anyone who cares to can spend all the time in the world going through the bag and finding socks that match. After a while, if the bag gets too big, Jay will get tired of it cluttering up the laundry area, and he will throw it away. And if eventually we need more socks, we just buy them. No doubt there are a myriad of ways to handle this that might teach responsibility and whatever else, but you know what? This method works just fine for us!

By the way, it's not that I don't care about living providently. I do. But there's more to manage here than just socks. There is only so much *time* to go around, especially in a big family, and I can't afford to spend that much precious time on *socks,* of all things. I just can't. Probably way-more-organized-and-wonderfully-together-woman can but that's not me. I'm way-wonderful-in-OTHER-things-woman, and I'm okay with that. Hey, I'm not greedy. I don't need to be everything. I'm very happy to be good at the things I'm good at, and I applaud you for the ones you're good at. I honestly admire your lovely, perfectly paired-up socks, and I learn from observing the ways you manage to do things. Your example teaches me and inspires me, and I love going to your classes and workshops. I appreciate listening to your advice on how-to's that I have no clue in the world about. Seriously, isn't it great that we're all so different? Life would be really boring if we all had the same gifts, talents, and abilities.

I LIKE it this way! It creates a natural system where we can *all* reach out to lift and bless each other, to help one another get closer to the level *we* might inherently be at. We all have something to give, so it's a great system if it's done right. We probably will "do it right" once we've created the Zion society that we know will exist in the near future. But we could start practicing it now, you know. Instead of being jealous on the one hand and critical on the other—of what other sisters are or aren't—why don't we all be grateful and give thanks for what we DO have, and then just help each other where we can? When enough people catch the vision of how a Zion people might interact day-to-day, and start making efforts in that direction, it's going to create something magical.

In the meantime, let's enjoy what we have that's wonderful about ourselves, and be sure not to judge others or be hard on them because they don't happen to share our gifts. Trust me, they have other ones. I absolutely believe that we can learn something important from *everyone.* Maybe even a useful new way (albeit a *last-ditch* way—try everything else first, okay?) of handling those life-sucking, unmatching socks!

Couldn't We Just Call It "Fast"ing?

I follow the law (with some *very slight* speeding
When driving to church, if I'm late for a meeting).

Getting to church on time can be rough for those of us with small children and/or big families! For our family, getting out the door on time was always a challenge regardless of what time church started, but it was probably the hardest the year it was at 8:30 A.M. I led the music in sacrament meeting, so we *had* to be on time. With nine of our kids at home, including three who were age three or younger, the only way for us to make it was for *every* item of clothing for each person to be laid out on the long window seat in the living room the night before. *Everything* had to be there—every pair of underwear, every sock, every hair bow, every bobby pin. And since it got so frustrating doing that on Saturday due to something or other that hadn't gotten put away properly the week before, we established the "church closet." Immediately after walking in the front door after church, the kids would take off every article of clothing, except for underwear, and we'd put it in the now emptied-out closet by the front door. Older kids could change in the bathroom and then put away their clothes. Socks went in shoes, shoes went in a laundry basket on the floor, neckties and bows went on the top shelf, and the rest got hung up. If something needed to be washed, I knew where it was and I could put it back. This worked great for us. Now we're down to three teens at home, who all manage to dress themselves and get out the door on Sundays, and we *still* call it the "church closet."

Can't-ser Treatment

There aren't many things
That are worse than a can't-ser!
Whatever you ask
Has a negative answer.

They'll tell you what's wrong with you,
What you *can't* do,
What's wrong with the world,
And your hopes and dreams, too.

"You *can't* like that person—just hear what they did.
You *can't* make a living at that.
You just *can't* imagine how bad it all is.
You *can't* think that dream won't go flat.

You *can't* say you really believe that—how dumb!
You *can't* think of wearing those clothes!
You *can't* understand just how awful she is."
You *can't* and you *can't* . . . on it goes . . .

They'll make you feel stressed,
And they'll leave you depressed,
As you drown in their doubt and debris.

I think it's more pleasant to NOT be un-can-ny.
I try to live life *can't-ser free*!

Not to say I'm always Little Miss Sunshine, but I am optimistic. However, I like Elder Neal A. Maxwell's comment best of all: "Naive optimism and pervasive pessimism are both to be avoided . . . Day in and day out, the gospel is the one thing that is most relevant, and we are *to be of good cheer*" (Neal A. Maxwell, *Deposition of a Disciple* [Salt Lake City: Deseret Book Co., 1976], 98; emphasis added).

Televulsion

I'd rather be a bookist than a seeist—
A-read-instead-of-sit-and-watch-TVist.
I think most studies find
That it's better for your mind,
And for sure, the way that I would rather be-ist!

[I've always been one who passionately adores books!]

Dr. Sue Hears a "Who?!"

They'd just been released, so who'd have that calling?
Somebody amazing. That job seemed appalling
To someone like me, who could surely not do it.
I had such respect for the ones who'd been *through* it.
A calling like that would simply undo me.
"Hi, Bishop. I'm here." His eyes went right through me.
You'd think that his look and his manner would clue me.
But I was in shock, then panicked, then gloomy
At what he asked next! I stammered,
"Who, ME??????????!"

Someone amazing
Is something I'm NOT!
The work still got done, though.
I guess I forgot
That whom the Lord calls,
Then the Lord qualifies.
But when it was *me*,
It was quite a surprise!

Most of us have had experiences similar to this in one way or another. I had one years ago, when I was a mommy with a five-year-old, a two-and-a-half-year-old, and a new baby at home. I had gone to Young Women's one particular week, because I had been asked to fill in for one of the teachers. I sat there with baby Eric on my lap, feeling overwhelmed just hearing about all the activities, programs, and events going on in our ward's Young

Women's program. At that time, each member of a Young Women presidency also served as a class advisor so she could get to know the girls that much better, and this seemed especially daunting to me. I remember clearly that when I left that day, I was shaking my head in wonder at all that those women did. I also thought about how very wise it was to have a Young Women's president with only one older teenager left at home, so she could have the time to devote to her calling.

I was stunned when, the very next Sunday, the bishop called *me* to serve as our ward's Young Women's president! Actually, *stunned* is probably a weak word for what I felt, but I'm not sure what the right word is. Let's just say I couldn't have been much more surprised if he had told me I was about to be called as our ward's next bishop! I had been the Young Women's president in another ward and had loved it, but I could hardly believe I was being called to this busy, demanding position right now.

I'm sure I didn't even *begin* to do what some sisters might have been able to accomplish in that calling. But I did have two amazing counselors, Donna London and Bobbi Nielsen, and even the thought of who they were and all they did still amazes me today. We somehow managed, and I was in that calling for a few years. I could easily share some ways, right off the top of my head, in which my life was blessed—and is still blessed today—from serving in that calling. Of course, leaders

are placed in certain positions so that those they serve might be blessed. I hope our girls knew they were loved, and felt inspired and encouraged to live temple-worthy lives, and to seek closeness to the Lord. It *is* true, though, that when we're doing what we can, even if everything isn't done as well as someone else might have done it, we're blessed too. And it never ceases to amaze me how the Lord so sweetly accepts our widow's mite of an offering, when it *is* all we have. It can seem so very inadequate to us, and yet He still blesses our efforts for the benefit of everyone involved.

Another reason we should never judge others for how they serve in their callings is because we don't truly know their abilities and circumstances. There have been many times when I've watched someone performing a certain assignment, realizing that if I was the one doing it, the outcome wouldn't be nearly as good, because it wasn't something I knew how to make happen very well, even though I would prayerfully do my best.

Maybe instead of being disappointed or even upset with the job someone is doing, we could pray for them. And not just say a prayer for them, but seek and wait and desire and reach until we actually connect with Heaven. Then we could seek for a blessing of strength or comfort or insight for that person, and keep at it. If we feel prompted to do something that will help or bless them—something where we don't overstep any bounds—then we could do that. That is how we sustain and support each other. Judging and criticism do absolutely nothing to help a person fulfill his or her calling. But praying for someone and seeking to lift and encourage that person can indeed bring power and peace and strength to that person—and to the giver. It's one way we can start pulling together and becoming of one heart and one mind. We're going to be doing that anyway, at some point not too far off. We might as well start practicing now to spread some blessings and strength around in the meantime, don't you think? And maybe, if it catches on, someone might even start praying for you!

Naptime for Mommy

(Something which, when you have a big family, is just an amusing wish!)

One tired mommy, trying to take a nap—
Up the night before with a baby on her lap.
Now the sickly baby's fine but Mom can't stay awake.
Hopes to sleep a little in a sixty-minute break.

In comes a cub scout, just about to go.
First he needs a treat to share (forgot to tell 'er, though).

One tired mommy, trying to sleep again.
She has started drifting off upon her pillow, when
In comes a teenager—wants to use a car.
Says that he'll be back by five, not going very far.

One tired mommy, stretched out on the bed,
In comes a daughter with a boo-boo on her head.
Only mommy's kiss can fix it; nothing else will do.
Mommy kisses boo-boo, sends her out then with a *shoo*.

"Mo-om!" yells a tattler. "He called me a booger!
She turned TV on again, and he knocked down the sugar!"

One tired mommy, resting all alone.
In comes a teenage girl who needs the cordless phone!

One tired mommy, tries again to doze.
Different daughter leaves for work, needs cash before she goes.

One tired mommy, sleeping on her back.
In peeks a ten-year-old, through just a little crack.
"Mom, are you asleep? Will you type my book report?"
"Later," mumbles Mommy since her naptime's getting short.

One tired mommy, feeling awfully droopy.
In comes a two-year-old: "Huwwy! I go poopy!"
Mommy stumbles out of bed and helps him on the potty.
Waits for five long minutes, hears, "I'm ready for karate!"

One exhausted mom drives her blue belt to the class.
Starts to drive back home again, then thinks she'd better pass.

One happy mommy, as peaceful as can be,
Sleeping in the parking lot inside her SUV!

[Absolutely! The best naps ever!]

To Keep It Wholly

Happy Sabbath, special day! I love when Sunday's here!
I always feel so good at church—so reverent and sincere.
At home I'll have to catch up on my housework and TV,
So all my time at church is always really good for me.

Welcome, welcome, Sabbath morning! Now we rest from care.
(At least while we're at church, with all the talks and lessons there.)
Afterward, I REALLY need to study for my test!
But then I'll take a nap, so it can be a day of rest.

Sunday—day that's set apart for lots of one-day sales!
I wouldn't shop on Sunday, but it seems it never fails . . .
This sale is JUST today; I won't be gone that many hours.
I need to get materials for quilts as gifts for showers.
That's service, right? Then after shopping, I'll be pretty beat,
So I won't cook, this day of rest. I'll get fast food to eat.

Sundays are okay. At least my teachers aren't that boring.
Sometimes talks in church, though, go so long I'm almost snoring.
Then when church is finally done, I'll try to not forget,
To get some scriptures read before I'm on the internet.

Sunday's here—the day I love the things I get to do!
I'll go to church and all of that, then afterward—woo hoo!
I'll watch today's big football game however long it takes,
Then restfully be underneath my car to do my brakes.

✿✿✿

Sacred Sabbath, day of rest♥ from every mortal care,*
May my time at church be blessed to feel His presence there.
Once I'm home, I'll do my best to rest from worldly things,
And enter then, into the rest ✪ a sacred Sabbath brings.

Sabbath—God's own chosen sign for those who choose
Him solely. ♦
Holy Sabbath, I will choose to keep this whole day wholly.✱
May I strive with my whole heart to worship, bless, and pray
This whole day long to make this be His wholly, holy day. ★

♥"True, Sunday is a day of rest, a change from the ordinary occupations of the week, but it is more than that. It is a day of worship, a day in which the spiritual life of man may be enriched. A day of indolence, a day of physical recuperation is too often a very different thing from the God-ordained day of rest. Physical exhaustion and indolence are incompatible with a spirit of worship. A proper observance of the duties and devotions of the Sabbath day will, by its change and its spiritual life, give the best rest that men can enjoy on the Sabbath day" (Joseph F. Smith, *Gospel Doctrine: Selections from the Sermons and Writings of Joseph F. Smith,* comp. John A. Widtsoe [Salt Lake City: Deseret Book Co., 1919], 242).

"The Sabbath is a holy day in which to do worthy and holy things. [Refraining] from work and recreation is important, but insufficient. The Sabbath calls for constructive thoughts and acts, and if one merely lounges about doing nothing on the Sabbath, he is breaking it. To observe it, one will be on his knees in prayer, preparing lessons, studying the gospel, meditating, visiting the ill and distressed, writing letters to missionaries, taking a nap, reading wholesome material, and attending all the meetings of that day at which he is expected" (Spencer W. Kimball, First Presidency Message, *Ensign,* Jan. 1978, 6).

"Over a lifetime of observation, it is clear to me that the farmer who observes the Sabbath day seems to get more done on his farm than he would if he worked seven days. The mechanic will be able to turn out more and better products in six days than in seven. The doctor, the lawyer, the dentist, the scientist will accomplish more by trying to rest on the Sabbath than if he tries to utilize every day of the week for his professional work. I would counsel all students, if they can, to arrange their schedules so that they do not study on the Sabbath. If students and other seekers after truth will do this, their minds will be quickened and the infinite Spirit will lead them to the verities they wish to learn. This is because God has hallowed his day and blessed it as a perpetual covenant of faithfulness" (James E. Faust, "The Lord's Day," *Ensign,* Nov. 1991, 33).

❇"Sweet is the day of sacred rest. No mortal care shall seize my breast" ("Sweet Hour of Prayer," *Hymns,* No. 147).

✪We can use the Sabbath as a time to grow closer to the Lord so we can enter into his rest.

Moroni 7:3 reads: "Wherefore, I would speak unto you that are of the church, that are the peaceable followers of Christ, and that have obtained a sufficient hope by which ye can enter into the rest of the Lord, from this time henceforth until ye shall rest with him in heaven." And D&C 84:24 clarifies: "Which rest is the fulness of his glory."

♦Observing the Sabbath signifies that we are God's people. It was chosen to be the sign of the covenant that exists between the Lord and His chosen people.

Exodus 31:12–13: "And the LORD spake unto Moses, saying, Speak thou also unto the children of Israel, saying, Verily my sabbaths ye shall keep: for it is a sign between me and you throughout your generations; that ye may know that I am the LORD that doth sanctify you."

"Recognition of a sacred Sabbath signifies the perpetual covenant existing between the Lord and His true followers. But if the sign of the covenant disappears, does the covenant itself cease to exist? Can we afford to be deprived of this covenant? Can we count the cost of such a loss?" (Mark E. Peterson, *The Way to Peace* [Salt Lake City: Deseret Book Co., 1969], 17).

★Exodus 20:8: "Remember the sabbath day, to keep it holy."

When you have children at home, trying to have everyone involved in Sabbath activities that are meaningful and appropriate, is both a challenge and something to aspire to. We have tried to focus our Sunday activities on the following:

- Worship—studying scriptures or lessons, having gospel-related activities or discussions, doing those things which would bring us closer to the Lord in some way.
- Service—the "visiting the sick" kind of service, not the "mow someone's lawn" type of service.
- Family—doing things to bring us closer to each other,

writing or emailing family members who are away from home, having simple dinners together and so on, versus having the football kind of family togetherness on Sunday.

We're always good about our "shalt nots" for Sunday, but we sometimes need to make a better effort to make sure that our time after church is *worshipful* and not just restful. It does take some thinking ahead of time about what to do. But some of the sweetest experiences we've had as a family have been on Sunday, so we know it's definitely worth the effort. Also, because of what the Sabbath is and because of what it signifies, it is essential for all of us to make sure our children know that we honor the Sabbath and *want* it to be holy.

*Special thanks to the ever-wonderful MEE, Mary Ellen Edmunds, for sharing her brilliant thought on keeping the Sabbath day "wholly," in our group discussion about Sunday worship.

Almost Senseless

(Yep! That sounds about right!)

A sense of direction is something that somehow, I lack.
If I've gotten there, that doesn't mean I can get back!
Just 'cause I'm here, won't mean I can get here again.
Usually, I'll make it, but can't always guarantee when.

For reasons unknown, I likewise have no sense of smell.
And yes, I taste food, although doubtless, I don't do it well.
Scent's an exotic and wonderfully strange-sounding mystery.
I'll know what it's like though someday, due to my future history.

A good sense of humor is one thing I've gratefully got.
In day-to-day living, that's something that helps quite a lot!
I *do* miss the other two senses, although I admit,
If given the choice of just one of the three,
A good sense of humor,
For sure,
Would be it.

Our Prophet, and Learning

You say I'm like a robot and I *can't* think for myself?
I keep my brain inside a jar and high upon a shelf?
I haven't joined the ranks of the enlightened, thinking people
Because I'm just a following, naive, unthinking sheeple?

That I don't *need* to think because the thinking has been done
For members of the Church like me, yes, each and every one?
That when the prophets speak, I'm just a mindless little minion?
Friend, you and I, it seems, have quite a difference of opinion!

I *think* that we have living prophets on the earth today!
I *think* I really *want* to know the things they have to say.

I *think* although I may be smart, informed, or educated,
Their counsel might be different than some views I may have
stated.

I *think* I'll reconsider my opinions and positions,
In light of their direction and inspired admonitions.

I *think* that I'll take counsel from a witness of the Savior,
Then *think* and pray about what I might change in my behavior.

I *think* it takes a lot more work and thinking to decide
To choose to follow after living prophets as a guide,
Than simply going blithely on a predetermined way,
Not hearkening to guidance we've been blessed with in our day.

When prophets speak, the thinking's done? For those with humble hearts,
That's when some deep and life-transforming thinking really starts!

I've often heard comments like the ones at the beginning of this poem, said about those of us who *want* to follow our living prophets because we really believe they are prophets. I got thinking about that, and realized how the whole "don't know how to think" claim was backwards. It takes effort and lots of serious and prayerful thinking to go through the process of hearing and determining how to apply the words of our living prophets, and of those who speak under the prophets' direction with words of counsel and guidance in General Conferences. How blessed we are by all these inspired messages! Like me, I'm sure you sometimes notice how unsettling things can get in the world today, and you whisper gratefully, "Thank you, Heavenly Father, for allowing us to have prophets living in our own time, to guide us through all this!"

Here are some favorite quotes and scriptures about prophets.

"The greatest of all scripture which we have in the world today is current scripture. What the mouthpiece of God says to his children is scripture. It is his word and his will and his law made manifest through scripture, and I love it more than all other" (Henry D. Moyle, BYU tri-stake fireside address, Jan. 1963; quoted in A. Theodore Tuttle, "What Is a Living Prophet," *Ensign,* July 1973).

"The most important prophet, so far as we are concerned, is the one who is living in our day and age. This is the prophet who has today's instructions from God to us today. God's revelation to Adam did not instruct Noah how to build the ark. Every generation has need of the ancient scripture plus the current scripture from the living prophet" (Ezra Taft Benson, "First Presidency Message: Fourteen Fundamentals in Following the Prophet," *Liahona,* June 1981, 1).

"If you want to know what the Lord has for this people at the present time, I would admonish you to get and read the discourses that have been delivered at this conference, for what these brethren have spoken by the power of the Holy Ghost is the mind of the Lord, the will of the Lord, the voice of the Lord, and the power of God unto salvation" (Harold B. Lee, "'Stand Ye in Holy Places,'" *Ensign,* July 1973, 121).

D&C 68:4: "And whatsoever they shall speak when moved upon by the Holy Ghost shall be scripture, shall be the will of the Lord, shall be the mind of the Lord, shall be the word of the Lord, shall be the voice of the Lord, and the power of God unto salvation."

"I hope you will get your copy of the [General Conference issue of the *Ensign*] and underline the pertinent thoughts and keep it with you for continual reference. No text or volume outside the standard works of the Church should have such a prominent place in your personal library shelves" (Spencer W. Kimball, 14 May 1968, in *Living Prophets for a Living Church* (manual), 1974, 92).

"I hope that we shall ponder with subdued feelings the [conference] talks to which we have listened. I hope that we will quietly reflect on the wonderful things we have heard . . . The test will come in the application of the teachings given . . . In our family home evenings I hope we will discuss with our children these things and let them taste the sweetness of the truths we have enjoyed. And when the *Ensign* magazine comes out in November, with all of the conference messages, please don't just throw it aside with the comment that you have heard it all, but read and ponder the various messages" (Gordon B. Hinckley, "'An Humble and a Contrite Heart,'" *Ensign,* Nov. 2000, 88–89).

AddledEssence

Child-turning-into-adult-in-between-ager,
Often-don't-care-if-their-bedroom-is-clean-ager,

Happy-to-live-on-a-pizza-cuisine-ager,
Soon-will-forever-need-more-gasoline-ager,

May-be-obsessed-with-routines-of-hygiene-ager,
Think-that-their-prom-should-include-limousine-ager,

Sometimes-appear-to-be-king-or-the-queen-ager,
Might-judge-themselves-by-absurd-magazine-ager,

Not-very-often-described-as-serene-ager,
Sifting-and-sorting-sublime-from-obscene-ager,

Making-us-wonder-should-we-intervene-ager,
Even-despite-what-they-do, don't-demean-ager,

Need-friends-and-family-upon-which-to-lean-ager,
Having-to-figure-out-what-does-life-mean-ager,

Some-just-as-valiant-as-this-world-has-seen-ager,
Fun-although-difficult-time-of-a-teenager.

Even though I enjoyed my teenage years, I wouldn't want to be a teenager again for anything, would you? Especially these days! Our kids certainly live in a different world than the one we grew up in. They have so much to deal with every single day. You don't have to spend very long on a high school or even middle school campus to see a little of what they're up against. They are, as President Hinckley put it, "growing up in a worldly environment that is laden with immorality and filth of every kind" (Gordon B. Hinckley, "We Have a Work to Do," *Ensign*, May 1995, 87). President Hinckley also described our world as a place "where filth, sleaze, pornography, and their whole evil brood are sweeping over us as a flood" (Gordon B. Hinckley, "Stand Up for Truth," BYU Devotional, 17 Sept. 1996).

How will our youth make it through this? How will they manage to have the strength, spirituality, courage, and power to overcome evil so great that it is "comparable in wickedness to the days of Noah, when the Lord cleansed the earth by flood"? (Ezra Taft Benson, *The Teachings of Ezra Taft Benson* [Salt Lake City: Deseret Book Co., 1988], 104–5).

In May 1981, the Young Men General Presidency stated, "You are going to accomplish the seemingly impossible because you are on His errand. Your generation will fight the greatest army of Satanic hosts ever assembled. You will be severely outnumbered. You will need a deep and abiding faith in Christ to survive—and you will survive.

The Lord and His servants will triumph, we do know that" (*Church News,* 9 May 1981; quoted in *New Era*, Apr. 1984, 14). How can our young people be expected to "accomplish the seemingly impossible," as they fight against "the greatest army of Satanic hosts ever assembled" where they "will be severely outnumbered"? What is out there that could possibly help them do all this?

We are, sisters. *We* are. We can and will help them through this because *WE are something special!* Not just a "unique and special child of God" kind of special, but a "noble birthright" and a "royal generation" kind of special. That's who we are. And it is who our youth are—a special, chosen generation, the "finest generation that has come to earth" (Richard G. Scott, "Do What is Right," BYU Devotional, 3 Mar., 1996), "among the most illustrious spirits to be born into mortality in any age of the world" (Harold B. Lee, *Happiness through Faith in Jesus Christ* [family home evening manual, 1977–78], 34).

We are all of the generation that has been saved to come forth at this time. And if you think this has always been said to every generation who happened to be coming up next, to inspire them or help them want to be good, you're mistaken. It hasn't. It has only been said to this one, because that is *who we are!* Let me share a few quotes with you.

President Joseph Fielding Smith (1970): "Our young people . . . are the nobility of heaven, a choice and chosen generation who have a divine destiny. Their spirits have been reserved to come forth in this day when the gospel is on the earth, and when the Lord needs valiant servants to carry on his great latter-day work" (Joseph Fielding Smith, *Conference Report*, Apr. 1970, 6).

President Harold B. Lee (1973): "I say to you, youth of the noble birthright, in your veins there runs the purest blood there is upon this earth today. You have been raised up for this time, the choicest that have lived on the earth. . . . Youth of the noble birthright, I say to you, 'Be loyal to the royal within you!" (Harold B. Lee, "To the Youth of the Church," in *The Teachings of Harold B. Lee*, ed. Clyde J. Williams [Salt Lake City: Deseret Book Co., 1996], 74).

President Spencer W. Kimball (1976): "We are rearing a royal generation—thousands of whom sit with us here tonight—who have special things to do" (Spencer W. Kimball, "Boys Need Heroes Close By," *Ensign,* May 1976, 45).

President Ezra Taft Benson (1988): "All through the ages the prophets have looked down through the corridors of time to our day. Billions of the deceased and those yet to be born have their eyes on us. Make no mistake about it—you are a marked generation. There has never been more expected of the faithful in such a short period of time as there is of us. . . . You are a royal generation. The heavenly grandstands are cheering you on. . . . Rise up, O youth of Zion!" (Ezra Taft Benson, "In His Steps," *Ensign*, Sept. 1988, 2).

President Gordon B. Hinckley (1992, 1995): "Truly, my dear young friends, you are a chosen generation. I hope you will never forget it. I hope you will never take it for granted. . . . You of this generation, this chosen generation, this royal priesthood, . . . you cannot with impunity follow practices out of harmony with values you have been taught. I challenge you to rise above the sordid elements of the world about you" (Gordon B. Hinckley, "A Chosen Generation," *Ensign*, May 1992, 70). "I love the youth of the Church. I have said again and again that I think we have never had a better generation than this" (Gordon B. Hinckley, "This is the Work of the Master," *Ensign*, May 1995, 70).

Thomas S. Monson (2001): "You, the youth of the Church, are a glorious group, a chosen generation" (Thomas S. Monson, "First Presidency Message: A Message to the Youth of the Church," *Ensign*, Feb. 2001, 2–3).

I hope you caught the fact that *six prophets of the Lord,* beginning in 1970, have all borne testimony of the nobility of this generation. At this time in the history of the world, we are here to do a great work—to do something in particular. We need to make sure we actually know what that is, since that would make it a little easier for us to go and do it! Here are a just a few comments about that, from the time some of us were "the youth," until now:

President Harold B. Lee (1973): "You have been raised up for this time . . . to prepare for the coming of the Lord, which may not be far away, maybe closer than any of us know" (Harold B. Lee, "To the Youth of the Church," 74). "Be prepared to become leaders in that glorious millennial day when Christ himself will reign as King of Kings and Lord of Lords" (Harold B. Lee, Lesson 29: "The Second Coming," *Young Women Manual 1* [2002], 125).

President Ezra Taft Benson (1988): "For nearly six thousand years, God has held you in reserve to make your appearance in the final days before the Second Coming of the Lord. . . . While our generation will be comparable in wickedness to the days of Noah, when the Lord cleansed the earth by flood, there is a major difference this time. It is that God has saved for the final inning some of his strongest children, who will help bear off the Kingdom triumphantly. And that is where you come in, for you are the generation that must be prepared to meet your God" (Ezra Taft Benson, *Teachings,* 104–5).

The First Presidency (2001): "We pray for each of you. May you keep your minds and bodies clean from the sins of the world so you can do the great work that lies before you. We pray that you will be worthy to carry on the responsibilities of building the kingdom of God and preparing the world for the Second Coming of the Savior" ("Message from the First Presidency," in *For the Strength of Youth* [2001], 2–3).

Yes, we are here, every member of the Church—whether rich or poor, married or single, with or without children—to prepare the world for the Second Coming of the Savior. That is what He has sent us here to do. We first start by preparing ourselves for the coming of the Savior. Then we can teach our youth how to do it. We can't just point them in a direction and say, "Okay, that's where you need to go! So, go on now. Good luck!" We need to faithfully follow our Savior until we truly find Him ourselves, and then we will be able to look our youth in the eyes with a smile, put a loving arm around their shoulders, and say, "Come, follow me. We can walk the path that follows Christ together." We need to *show* them what to do and how to do it.

I'm not exactly sure what we will be asked to do to prepare the world for His Second Coming, but we know the Lord will help us do it. Someone like me certainly wouldn't know much about all the specifics it will involve! But I do know how it starts. It starts by us RISING UP, sisters—by our rising up and pulling ourselves up out of the filth and decadence of the world, so He can work with us. As long as we love the things of this world, such as the impure forms of "entertainment" that engulf us today, more than we love the Lord, we're basically on our own. He doesn't want it to be that way! But sometimes *we* apparently do, when we continue to choose the profane, impure, vulgar, immoral, and unclean instead of Him, not even realizing how much joy, beauty, comfort, goodness, peace, strength, healing, knowledge, and heavenly assistance we are passing up by making these seemingly insignificant choices.

But once we finally decide to choose the Lord instead of the darkness of the world, our lives will begin to open up, and we will eventually be led to such love, beauty, and majesty that we can hardly believe it's real—and that it's for *us*. That's just part of the blessing that awaits those who choose to be faithful followers of the Savior, who seek Him until they find Him. Once we've done that, we will be prepared to do what He has sent us here to do, and we will be able to show others around us, especially our youth, how to do it too.

Now, I don't want anyone to read this and go, "Great. One more thing I'm not good enough at. One more thing I'm supposed to do, when I can't even get through the things I'm trying to do now!" and be all mopey and depressed about it. This isn't like that. Let me tell you a little story to illustrate what I mean.

My husband, Jay, is amazing. I try not to talk about him too much because I don't want anybody to hate me, like the kid who always brags about the size of his swimming pool or his dad's expensive car. So even though this story does show off a little of my husband's amazingness, I hope you'll let it go this time. Every Sunday morning, Jay makes dinner in the Crockpot so I can have a day off from cooking. I like to cook, but after the first ten to fifteen thousand meals or so, it starts to get a little old. So on Sundays, Jay almost always makes a roast with small potatoes (skin on), and maybe carrots for us. He spices it up and it's *so* yummy. Since it's normally what we have on Sunday because it's simple but so good, one or the other of our kids will sometimes ask, "Are we having normal dinner today?"

Well, one week, we weren't having normal dinner, because we'd decided to have a ham we'd bought on sale around Easter. That Sunday, Jay got up early, went out to the freezer, got the frozen-solid ham, and put it in the Crockpot on HIGH. (Sorry to interrupt this exciting story about frozen ham here, but I just have to stop a second to comment on Jay getting up early that Sunday morning. His getting up early wasn't about making a ham, or about it being Sunday, or anything like that. Jay always gets up early in the morning! Oh, how he *loves* the morning! I call him my sunshine-in-the-morning boy. He gets up at 5:10 A.M., five days a week, so he can play racquetball before he picks the kids up from seminary at 7:00 A.M., to drive them over to the high school. I also get up pretty early, but it wouldn't be my first choice, if it was just up to me with no other considerations. In fact, I doubt that it would be in my top 1000! I get up so I can get the kids off to seminary. Nine kids' worth of seminary—our youngest just started this year—has gotten me somewhat used to waking up early, like those silly, bright-and-sunny morning people do. But Mr. Sunshine? Despite when I get up, he's usually already up, being busy and doing things, like he was this particular Sunday morning.)

Okay, we can go back to the frozen-solid ham now. We weren't eating until many hours later, so the fact that the ham was frozen solid didn't matter. It would be done in plenty of time. Jay put in his spices—his delicious *hot* spices—and started it all cooking. When it was almost time to eat, I went to take the ham out, because I'm often the one who makes the gravy. I took the Crockpot lid off, then stopped and tried to figure out what I was looking at. The skin of the ham was hard and wrinkled-up and looked . . . strange. As I tried to stick a meat fork into it to put it on a serving dish, I finally realized what the problem was. The ham was still sealed in the plastic that was on it when we bought it at the store! Because it had been frozen, the ham was white and frosty-looking on the outside. Jay had gotten busy with the other things he was preparing for dinner, and then just plunked the frosty ham into the Crockpot, without remembering that it was still sealed in plastic!

We had to cut the plastic off the ham, which was kind of a pain, since the ham was very hot. Getting all the plastic off was pretty messy, and then, although the ham was still basically edible, the meat hadn't absorbed any of Jay's yummy, spicy flavors that we all love so much. But it was mostly okay, and we all enjoyed a good-natured laugh over it. (By the way, Jay said to tell you he's glad to know his ineptness can bless the sisters of the Church.)

Now, what if I had said, "I think that maybe next time, it might be good to take the plastic off first," and Jay had moped, "Great. Just one more thing for me to do. I make dinner, but that's not good enough. I have to do this plastic thing, too!" "Wait!" I would explain. "Just listen for a minute. You don't have to do *more.* You only have to do what you're doing now a little differently. It's actually *easier* to take the plastic off first. Plus, believe it or not, the ham will taste even better than it did with the plastic on!"

I hope you see the point. I do realize that what we were talking about before sounds like just one more thing to do, but what I am suggesting is that this will actually make it much *easier* to do the things you're doing now that need to be done. And everything will be sweeter. You will love your loved ones more. They will be more drawn to you. Your life will feel lighter and more joyful, and so much more. Once you seek the Lord until you find Him, your world will change. It will become something that feels entirely different than what you're doing now. And the main point here is this: Most of us are already doing so many good and faithful things that we just need to make *a few simple adjustments,* like taking the plastic off. My belief is that, for most of us, our worlds will completely change if we:

1. Decide we're not going to partake of the impure things of the world anymore. I feel so strongly that due to the impure entertainment around us, most of us are missing out on so many spiritual things that could and should be ours. Sisters, what we watch, read, or look at doesn't have to be raunchy or disgusting to prevent us from having the companionship of the Holy Ghost. It only needs to be impure. Let me give you just one statement from *For the Strength of Youth* to consider. Ponder this simple little line for a while, and see what thoughts come to mind: "Do not participate in

entertainment that *in any way* presents immorality or violent behavior as acceptable" (p. 17; emphasis added).

Is nudity mentioned here? How about actual sexual content? No, neither of these items is specifically referred to here. This statement doesn't talk about acts of immorality being shown, but of entertainment "making what is wrong and evil look normal" (ibid). Violent behavior is mentioned in the same way.

If we truly adopted what it says here as our standard in order to have our lives be pure, how many primetime TV shows would we watch? (See M. Russell Ballard, "Let Our Voices Be Heard," *Ensign*, Nov. 2003, 16.)

What movies would we attend, buy, or rent? I have sometimes wondered what it would be like if the Savior sat down beside us, picked up the *TV Guide* and a handful of our DVDs, then gently and beseechingly asked, "Dearest, lovest thou these more than me?"

Sisters, we need to stop worrying so much about our lives being "perfect," and start paying attention to whether or not our lives are pure. Sheri Dew said it wonderfully in her book *Saying It Like It Is:* "The object of this life is not to become perfect. That comes later. The object of mortality is to become increasingly pure. Purity is a key to drawing upon the power of the Lord. Purity is always a characteristic of a true follower of Jesus Christ."

I would like to challenge you to consider doing an experiment of sorts, by going a week making a conscious effort to have your entertainment be more pure, whether it comes from TV, music, books, magazines, movies, or the internet. If you use the standard discussed above, you may find yourself with some extra time on your hands! See if you can feel the difference it makes in your life. Do you feel more peace? Can you sense the Spirit more easily? Do your prayers feel more meaningful? Does your heart feel more open to those around you? Do you just plain feel better inside?

Alma says it so well in Alma 32:35: "O then, is not this real? I say unto you, Yea, because it is light; and whatsoever is light, is good, because it is discernible, therefore ye must know that it is good."

Please try this out for yourself and see if it feels good. You may end up noticing spiritual influences all around about you that you hadn't been aware of before because they were being drowned out by your entertainment choices.

2. Determine to be obedient. Each of us can decide that we will do our best to keep the commandments and follow the counsel of the living prophets in our day. That *does not* mean we will frantically run around, trying to do ten zillion things on an endless list! It *does* mean we will always work on obeying Him, and will not intentionally break commandments or go against the Lord's counsel though His prophets just because that's what we really desire to do. It also means that if we do intentionally break a commandment, we will sincerely repent and work on doing better next time, instead of intending to keep on doing the same thing over and over because it happens

to be one of our favorite sins. And look, I'm not trying to tell you the specifics of what to do in your life. That's why we're given the gift of the Holy Ghost. If your life right now has many sins and issues to work on, the Lord will walk you through how to do that. But you must honestly *desire* to start to be obedient, even if a fuller obedience is difficult to achieve right now.

Also, we can do our best to learn to hear the voice of the Spirit, and then obey, obey, obey! This will be one of the main ways He'll be able guide our steps through the minefields of these dangerous days, and onto the path leading into His arms of love and safety.

3. Spend time *really praying*, instead of just saying prayers. Elder Richard G. Scott gives us some very useful information about our personal relationship with our Heavenly Father that can help us when we pray. Elder Scott explains that even though our Father in Heaven has created numberless worlds, we can still talk with Him personally because He is near and He is listening when we pray. He is a compassionate, understanding Father who never thinks we are too unworthy to pray. He looks upon each of us as a precious child whom He loves perfectly and wants to help, and He wants us to just talk to Him. (See Richard G. Scott, "Using the Supernal Gift of Prayer," *Ensign,* May 2007, 8–11.) If we think of our Heavenly Father in these terms when we pray, it can help us stop repeating the same words and phrases, and help us yearn with our souls to communicate with Someone who is nearby and listening

to every word, even more interestedly than a caring father here on earth would be.

And once our lives are pure and we are obedient, it can be helpful to seek to feel His nearness as we pray. It's important that we are already able to clearly recognize what the Spirit feels like, as well as how the peace that comes from the Lord feels. Then we can seek to feel that from Him as we draw close to Him in prayer. If we spend more quiet time, waiting, pondering, and searching for Him as we pray, it can help draw our hearts close to Him. In addition to whatever else we may pray about, we could work on not asking for things, but instead ask Him what we could do to become closer to Him. And then we can work on doing that.

Elder Scott further counsels in his address on prayer: "A key to improved prayer is to learn to ask the right questions" (ibid). What if you also asked your Heavenly Father if it's true that you are here at this time to help prepare the world for the Second Coming, as the latter-day prophets and the First Presidency have said? Replies to questions with "yes" or "no" answers are usually simpler to discern than those requiring more complex answers. And our questions about who we are and what we are here to do, may be ones He might particularly want to be able to answer clearly for us. Remember that discerning answers requires patience and practice, plus your personal purity and obedience make a difference in how much and how clearly you can receive replies through the Spirit.

If we spent much more time praying than we do now,

> we would learn so much more about prayer than can be expressed here. Aside from having our hearts be pure and obedient, spending much more time in prayer, seeking to truly connect with Heaven, might be the most useful thing we could do for our souls. It can give us great understanding and strength, and ultimately can fill and bless us so much that our lives will feel refreshed and joyful.

Some of this may take a bit of sacrifice at first, but the great thing is, sacrificing what we might want to do, in order to do what He would want us to do ("Thy will, not mine"), is one way we show the Lord that we are serious about following Him. And it gets easier. In fact, overall, it will be so much easier than what you're doing now. Also, a peace will settle upon your heart, and you will feel right about the direction your life is taking, even if you haven't reaped all the rewards and blessings from it yet. Trust Him enough to believe that what He has said is true, and that incredible blessings are available in this lifetime if you stick with it.

Then, regardless of what happens, *press on and never stop.* His promises are true and they are sure! One day, you will reach a place that makes you marvel in wonder at the joy and sweetness in your life, if you will just stick with it, come what may. In times of trial, which will come to each and every one of us, including His faithful followers, press forward and *trust Him!* No matter what comes up, if you are doing your best to faithfully follow the Savior, it will be okay. At some point, you will become so close to Him that you will be blessed and filled to overflowing with His pure, sweet, healing love, but that time may not be as soon as you think it should be. Have the faith to trust that He won't let anything permanently destroy you (even though it might feel like that sometimes!) and that earth truly has no sorrow that Heaven cannot heal.

Remember that all things work together for the good of those that love the Lord, and that everything that happens in your life can be used by Him to bless you in one way or another. If you don't let the hard-to-bear experiences of life make you become bitter, they can give you compassion and understanding. They can be the refiner's fire to help purify you. They could also leave you feeling so broken and wounded that you're driven to seek the Lord and beg for the Savior to heal you. He can and does do that, even though it might not happen for you as immediately as you were hoping for. But once He does heal your heart, you will be left with an incredible adoration of your Savior, and a relationship with Him that you never had before. Your whole soul will overflow with gratitude for the circumstances that allowed you to be brought to that place.

Your Heavenly Father knows what He is doing in your life. He knows where you need to go and what will help you get there. Seek to exercise faith in His love and wisdom on your behalf, instead of being dragged through trials kicking and screaming. In these last days when Satan rages, the Lord needs us to learn to trust Him regardless of what is happening to us or around us. This is part of the process, and something very important that we need to know both for ourselves, and so that we can bear testimony of it to our youth from our own personal experiences. So hold on, and trust Heaven's promises!

Start now in simple ways to begin increasing your purity, prayer, and obedience, in place of some of what you're already doing. Doing this, combined with a desire to seek the Savior with all your heart, can help you be ready for His Second Coming. But whether His coming is very soon, or sometime much later, His coming close to YOU will be *whenever you are ready.* He tells us, "Draw near unto me and I will draw near unto you; seek me diligently and ye shall find me; ask, and ye shall receive; knock, and it shall be opened unto you" (D&C 88: 63); and "Verily, thus saith the Lord: It shall come to pass that every soul who forsaketh his sins and cometh unto me, and calleth on my name, and obeyeth my voice, and keepeth my commandments, shall see my face and know that I am" (D&C 93:1).

You can become filled with His love and His power. Through your example, you can be a shepherd to our youth as they desperately try to find their way through this darkened world. You can be a shining example of how to become what the Lord has asked us to be.

But please don't think you need to become a Sister Helaman, amassing a huge army of righteous latter-day warriors behind you or something like that. You don't. You only need to be an everyday Latter-day Saint woman who is pure, faithful, and willing to do the Lord's work in whatever your own circumstances are. Who knows? He may change those circumstances and direct you elsewhere, or He may not. His light needs to shine everywhere, from the highest mountaintops to the humblest abodes. Wherever you are, and in whatever you do, your testimony, your love, and your goodness can draw others to you who are seeking the light. That is one of the reasons *we* are here now, because we have what it takes to become filled with that light.

Let's RISE UP, sisters of Zion, rise up and be who we truly are! Heaven is counting on us. The seconds are counting down.

Let's rise up and courageously tell Satan's countless counterfeits, "Count me out, because I can be counted on to make my presence in these last days count!"

Follow Promptings Promptly

"Always follow promptings promptly."
That's a good expression.
Try to pay attention when you first feel an impression.
You *don't* need bolts of lightning that can split the ground apart,
But just a gentle whisper in your mind or in your heart.

Learning to hear the promptings of the Spirit is one of the most important and valuable life skills we can aspire to master. Then, once we begin to recognize when the Spirit is prompting us, our aim should be to follow that guidance as quickly as seems appropriate. President Thomas S. Monson counseled, "We watch. We wait. We listen for that still, small voice. When it speaks, wise men and women obey. Promptings of the Spirit are not to be postponed" (Thomas S. Monson, *Live the Good Life* [Salt Lake City: Deseret Book Co., 1988], 59). This vital communication with Heaven comes quietly. Most often it's as hushed as a whisper, or as muted as a thought just on the edge of our minds.

As President Boyd K. Packer explained, "The Spirit does not get our attention by shouting or shaking us with a heavy hand. Rather it whispers. It caresses so gently that if we are preoccupied we may not feel it at all. Occasionally, it will press just firmly enough for us to pay heed. But most of the time, if we do not heed the gentle feeling, the Spirit will withdraw and wait until we come seeking and listening" (Boyd K. Packer, "The Quest for Spiritual Knowledge," *New Era*, Jan. 2007, 2–7).

"Always follow promptings promptly."
What else are they for?
A prompting's not a thing to just take lightly or ignore.
Remember it's a message from the Lord, and not a whim,
And those who follow promptings promptly
Follow them to *Him*.

Even though promptings may *feel* small, they are always of importance in our lives. As Elder Richard Scott said: "You have been prompted by the Spirit about private things the Lord wants you to do something about. . . . They are a personal message of the Lord to you" (Richard G. Scott, "Trust in the Lord," *Ensign,* May 1989, 35). Because promptings are typically so gentle and even subtle, it can be hard for us to grasp the reality that they are indeed personal messages of the Lord to us, our private and personal messages from Heaven! Promptings of the Spirit are a small and simple means by which great things are brought to pass (see Alma 37:6). In order for us to continue receiving these messages from Him, we need to pay attention to them. And once we receive them, we need to diligently do what they instruct us to do. President Packer declared, "Ignore or disobey these promptings, and the Spirit will leave you. It is your choice—your agency" (Boyd K. Packer, "The Gift of the Holy Ghost," *Friend,* July 1995).

"Always follow promptings promptly."
Make a firm decree
To try to follow right away, and do it faithfully.
Times when you don't want to stop and go do what it is,
Remember that the still, small voice the Spirit brings is *His*.

It would be so wonderful if we each made a commitment to always try to follow the promptings we receive. Although it's not always easy to follow, this heavenly guidance tutors us in how to live like the Savior would, and isn't that our goal? Elder F. Enzio Busche explained: "It takes courage and commitment to follow the promptings of the Spirit because they may frighten us as they lead us to walk along new paths, sometimes paths that no one has walked before, paths of the second mile, of acting totally differently from how worldly people act. For instance, we may be prompted to smile when someone offends us, to give love where others give hate, to say thank you where others would not find anything to be thankful for, to accept jobs that others would be too proud to do, to apologize where others would defend themselves, and to do all the seemingly crazy things that the Spirit prompts a righteous, honest, listening heart to do" (F. Enzio Busche, "The Only Real Treasure," *New Era*, Dec. 1979, 9). What a gift it is to have personal instruction and training to help us become like our Lord!

"Follow promptings promptly."
They are sent because we need them.
The heavens might as well be silent if we do not heed them.
One thing you can *count* on is they lead to truth and light,
And everything they ask of you is something good and right.

Most of us have received promptings from the Spirit during times of great danger and during times when we desperately needed the Lord's counsel. While these kinds of promptings are important, there is an even greater need for divine promptings in our normal, day-to-day lives. On a daily basis—even moment to moment—the Lord will guide our steps, comfort us, and teach us, if we will but let Him. President Joseph F. Smith said, "[All have] the privilege to exercise these gifts and these privileges in the conduct of [their] own affairs, in bringing up [their] children in the way they should go, and in the management of [their] business . . . It is [their] right to enjoy the spirit of revelation and of inspiration to do the right thing, to be wise and prudent, just and good in everything [they do] . . . for their personal guidance to strengthen their faith, and to encourage them in works of righteousness, . . . It is the right and privilege of every man, every woman, and every child who has reached the years of accountability, to enjoy the spirit of revelation" (Joseph F. Smith, *Gospel Doctrine,* 34–35, 41–42).

Most importantly, we should understand that as we live worthy of, seek for, and receive promptings of the Spirit, we will be led to do that which is righteous and good. President Ezra Taft Benson shared Brigham Young's dream of Joseph Smith, where he had a message for the Saints on this very subject: "Several years after Joseph Smith was martyred, he appeared to President Brigham Young. Hear his message: 'Tell the people to be humble and faithful, and be sure to keep the spirit of the Lord and it will lead them right. Be careful and not turn away the small still voice; it will teach you what to do and where to go'" (Ezra Taft Benson, "Seek the Spirit of the Lord," *Ensign,* Apr. 1988, 2).

"Always follow promptings promptly."
Learn to hear the Spirit.
Think of how it feels so you will know it when you hear it.
Learning how to hear the Lord, through things He asks of you,
Is one of the important things in life you're here to do.

We lead such busy lives these days! There are so many places to be, so many things to do, and so much that is important and even crucial to our eternal well-being. However, learning how to communicate with our Father in Heaven through prayer and through the impressions He sends us is of unique importance, since that will assist us in accomplishing the other necessities of our lives. President Harold B. Lee instructed, "The most important thing you can do is to learn to talk to God. Talk to Him as you would talk to your father, for He is your Father, and He wants you to talk to Him. He wants you to cultivate ears to listen, when He gives you the impressions of the Spirit to tell you what to do. If you learn to give heed to the sudden ideas which come to your minds, you will find those things coming through in the very hour of your need. If you will cultivate an ear to hear these promptings, you will have learned to walk by the spirit of revelation" (Lee, *Teachings*, 130). Prayer is how we talk to God. The promptings of the Spirit are how He most often talks to us.

"Always follow promptings promptly."
They're an invitation
To learn that what a prompting brings is whispered revelation.
Learn to follow every prompting, even if it's small.
It has its purpose, plus you'll learn to hear your Shepherd's call.

The quiet promptings of the Spirit may sometimes feel insignificant, but as President Joseph F. Smith said, "Revelation comes to us most often through the still, small voice of the Spirit" (Joseph F. Smith, in *Teachings of Presidents of the Church: Joseph F. Smith,* Chapter 20, "Yield to the Promptings of the Spirit"). The critical issue here is learning to hear and understand the voice of the Lord through the promptings of the Spirit. He will often instruct us in us small things. Some of these promptings may, if followed, simply make our day come together easier, or they might help us do something fairly minor for someone else. As Elder Neal A. Maxwell explained, "Promptings for us to do good come from the Holy Ghost. . . . Even the moments that seem humdrum are full of possibilities. Nothing is really routine. We must look carefully, therefore, at the seemingly small moments. Even small acts and brief conversations count . . . in the constant shaping of souls" (Neal A. Maxwell, "The Pathway of Discipleship," *Ensign,* Sept. 1998, 7). However, even promptings that seem trivial to us are still important. "I am extremely thankful for a most loving Heavenly Father who has given us the gift of the Holy Ghost . . . I will continue to pay attention to the promptings I receive, no matter how trivial or inconvenient the situation may seem" (Polly Daw, in "Latter-day Saint Voices," *Ensign*, Aug. 2002, 68–71). In addition to the obvious purposes of promptings, they help us to learn to hear and understand the Lord's voice. Elder Joseph B. Wirthlin stated, "The Shepherd calls to each of us today. Will we recognize the voice of the Son of God? Will we follow Him?" (Joseph B. Wirthlin, "'Follow Me,'" *Ensign,* May 2002, 15).

"Always follow promptings promptly."
Make a holy choice
To always do what He reminds you through the Spirit's voice.
As we learn to follow, then that voice gets ever clearer,
We can hear it better since we're drawing ever nearer.

Our doing even the small and simple things we are prompted to do through the Spirit brings us ever closer to the Lord. We also begin to understand the Spirit more clearly as we actively seek promptings with the intent to follow, bless, and obey. Instead of only being able to discern a positive or peaceful feeling about something, or a feeling contrary to that, we will begin to receive clear impressions about specific things. But the Lord is not sending us anything different now; He is still speaking to us through the Holy Ghost. It is our ability to *understand* the impressions that has increased. President Packer points out, "You can learn now, in your youth, to be led by the Holy Ghost. As an Apostle I listen now to the same inspiration, coming from the same source, in the same way, that I listened to as a boy. The signal is much clearer now" (Boyd K. Packer, "Prayers and Answers," *Ensign,* Nov. 1979, 19).

When you follow promptings, you're sometimes Heaven's hand,
And you'll be sent to someone else for what the Lord has planned.
When *you're* what He sends them as the answer to their prayers,
You'll see the way *your* life was blessed, while you were blessing *theirs.*

Have you ever done something for someone and been left with a warm, wonderful feeling inside? I'll never forget a sweet and simple truth shared in sacrament meeting years ago by a twelve-year-old young man named Dustin Glauser. He gave a pretty standard little talk about service and helping others, and then said this: "You know that good feeling you get inside after you've helped someone else? I think that's probably Heavenly Father's way of saying, 'Thank you.'" And so it is. When we're directed to bless someone else's life, our own lives are also enriched and blessed. Elder Busche declared, "I know that the individual who concentrates, as first priority in his life, on efforts to listen to the still, small voice all the time, and learns to obey that voice, will not only have a blessed life for himself, but he will be also a constant source of strength to his fellowmen" (F. Enzio Busche, "Powerfully Strong," *New Era,* Mar. 1989, 4). We truly are the hands of Heaven as we seek to know and do what things the Savior might do if He were in our circumstances.

"What if I can't tell if it's the Spirit or it's me?"
You can learn to sort it out by searching earnestly.
Ask your Heavenly Father if He'll help you recognize
When it's you, and when they're really promptings or replies.

When we express our earnest desire to our Heavenly Father to learn to understand the Spirit, He will help us learn how to do that. He *wants* us to be able to connect with Him and receive direction at His hand, but we may need to work on putting our lives in a state where we are better able to receive and understand the Holy Ghost's promptings. Elder Joseph B. Wirthlin stated, "I fear that some members of the Lord's Church 'live far beneath our privileges' with regard to the gift of the Holy Ghost. Some are distracted by the things of the world that block out the influence of the Holy Ghost, preventing them from recognizing spiritual promptings. Brothers and sisters, do we turn away the still, small voice? . . . Do we allow influences into our homes that drive the Spirit from our homes? . . . Much of the entertainment of the world is offensive to the Holy Ghost. Surely we should not watch movies or television shows that are filled with violence, vulgar language, and immorality" (Joseph B. Wirthlin, "The Unspeakable Gift," *Ensign*, May 2003, 26). In order to learn how to hear the Lord's voice, we could start by asking Him how we can be more in tune with His Spirit. "The Spirit speaks in such a still, small voice that it might be unrecognized if one is not spiritually in tune. Through sincere prayer, we can ask Heavenly Father to give us the ability to recognize the sweet promptings of the Spirit and the courage to follow that guidance." ("Questions and Answers," Question: 'I have difficulty distinguishing between promptings of the Spirit and my own personal feelings. How can I tell the difference?" *Ensign,* Mar. 2007, 58–61). As we begin to do those things that will help us draw closer to Him, we can continue to pray and ask for His help in learning to hear His voice. He will help us learn to hear Him! As Elder Dieter F. Uchtdorf explained, "To receive knowledge from the Holy Ghost, we must ask Heavenly Father for it. We must trust that God loves us and that He will help us to recognize the promptings of the Holy Ghost" (Dieter F. Uchtdorf, "The Power of a Personal Testimony," *Ensign,* Nov. 2006, 37–39).

Notice how it feels in places where the Spirit's there.
When you feel a peace or "rightness," also be aware.
Desiring to follow Christ and seeking for the good,
Allows the still, small voice to be more clearly understood.

One of the blessings of following the Savior and keeping the commandments is that doing those things can often bless us with feelings of the Spirit when our heart is right. Other things that can allow us to feel the Spirit are searching and pondering the scriptures and serving others, which we discussed earlier. Everyone has probably been in a wonderful sacrament meeting and in other circumstances when testimony is borne in various ways, where the Spirit is present in abundance. Doing anything that brings the Spirit and being in places where the Spirit will be present are important ways to learn how to recognize what Heaven's promptings feel like. "When you are in a situation where you are positive that the Spirit is present—such as a testimony meeting, during a musical number, after receiving a blessing, and so on—take note of how you feel. Write down your thoughts and feelings. This way you learn what the Spirit feels like, as it can be different for you than for someone else. As you learn to recognize this feeling, the second step is putting yourself in a place where you can receive revelation. This is why regular, meaningful prayer and scripture study are so vital—they keep us centered in a place where we can feel the Spirit" ("Questions and Answers"). Although the voice of the Spirit may not feel exactly the same for everyone, it is almost always accompanied a feeling of "rightness" or peace. Sister Ardeth G. Kapp said, "In your daily prayers you might ask, 'Father in Heaven, what can I do today to help in thy work?' You might simply ask, 'What should I do or not do to be . . . better?' If you listen carefully, thoughts will come into your mind, and you will be surprised at the guidance you will receive when you sincerely ask and then listen. . . . When you follow these promptings, a warm, good feeling will come over you, and you will know that what you are doing is right" (Ardeth G. Kapp, "Stand for Truth and Righteousness," *Ensign*, Nov, 1988, 93). In some ways, it's almost like the childhood game of Hot and Cold, where we're told we're getting *warm, warmer, hot!*, or *cold, colder, freezing!* That feeling of peace says we're getting warmer, and as we endeavor to follow the promptings as we understand them, we'll learn to tell the difference between being spiritually "hot" and spiritually "cold."

Then let that loving voice, which you will learn to understand,
Reach down to touch your mind and heart, then lead you by
the hand.
"I will follow promptings promptly!" Hold that in your heart.
You'll learn the way. Perhaps *today's* a perfect time to start!

The Lord is waiting for us to come to Him. He has already extended numberless invitations in a myriad of ways for us all to come and be blessed: "He inviteth them all to come unto him and partake of his goodness; and he denieth none that come unto him, black and white, bond and free, male and female; and he remembereth the heathen; and all are alike unto God, both Jew and Gentile" (2 Ne. 26:33). Following the promptings of the Spirit leads us to do those things that will bring us back into the loving presence of our Father and our Savior. President James E. Faust witnessed: "I further testify that I would rather have every person enjoy the Spirit of the Holy Ghost than any other association, for they will be led by that Spirit to light and truth and pure intelligence, which can carry them back into the presence of God" (James E. Faust, "The Gift of the Holy Ghost—A Sure Compass," *Ensign,* Apr. 1996, 2).

This is something we can all learn to do. This is something we were *created* to do! This is something that the Lord yearns for us to do. Why not start today? Why not start right now, in this very moment?

He is there.
He is listening.
He is waiting.
He will help.
He misses you.
He wants you to hear Him.
He wants you to come to Him.
Go.

Do the Following . . .

I think that we can *do* this if we just decide to try.
Regardless of our circumstances, there's no reason why
A single thing can block us or can stop us on our way—
Let's be the faithful followers of Jesus Christ today!

That doesn't mean we're "perfect," but we want to do His will,
And even when we falter, we will try to follow still.
We'll quickly make amends, and we will pray, explaining how
We're sorry we did wrong, but that we're following Him *now*.

Then, if we keep on doing that, we're going to be okay.
Let's *be* those faithful followers of Jesus Christ today!

So . . .
If we meet our old fiancé when we look a mess,
If we're at church with pantyhose all tucked up with our dress,
Or if we scrape a car that's parked, while driving through the fog,
Or we're locked out in just a robe, because we chased our dog,

Or if the day's so packed that dinner's just a frozen waffle,
Or we get called to school because our son was simply awful,
Or we rushed home to make some food to take, then no one
ate it,
Or teens won't come to family night because they say they hate it,

Or stains were on our shirt all day, although we didn't know it,
Or people who should love us rarely ever seem to show it,
Or if that same old thing that used to trip us up back then,
Has surfaced in our life, and needs repenting once again,

Or if we say an ugly word we wish we hadn't said,
Or if it seems so many are so very far ahead,
And we are barely on the path, just struggling hard to crawl,
While others there are running, and we'll *never* do it all,

Or friends have said some things about our life that just
aren't true,
Or everything seems awful, and we don't know what to do.

Despite whatever happens, or what anyone might say,
We *still* can choose to be His faithful followers today!
We might have things to deal with, but we still can keep the vision
That following the Lord—or not—is always *our* decision.

In certain situations, we might *not* have much to give,
But our desire to follow Christ can be the way we live.
We offer what we have to Him, and in our heart we say:
"I wish that it was more, but still, I'll follow Thee today."

And we may learn one day, that through His grace, our mite
sufficed!
Oh, sisters, we can DO this, so *today* let's follow Christ!

Well, that's it for now, then. I've loved having you here with me, and would love even more to hear from you! Email me anytime at victoriagunther@gmail.com, or go to my website at www.girlinawhirl.com. I'd really enjoy seeing you there and hearing what's going on with YOU. I just might write about it one of these days! Tell me about the best thing that's happening in your life right now, or your funny stories, favorite recipes, or anything else you have going on. I'd love to know more about you and how life is in your corner of the universe.

Also, I know that sometimes when I've read something by someone else, I form an impression of what I think that person is like. I hope that one thing you came away with from this book is that *we're all here to work together* and just help each other where we can with whatever we may happen to have. I hope I didn't make anyone feel like I think I'm something special or anything, just because this is my book. If there's one thing I excel at, it's in being average! It's one of my best qualities. And there are some areas of my life where being average is actually the goal I aspire to right now! Hey, we're all working on things of one kind or another. So let's just help and encourage each other.

I'm excited to meet you! Until then, be good, do good, and know that you are always very loved by your Heavenly Father and His Son.

XO,
Victoria
www.girlinawhirl.com

About the Author

Victoria Gunther earned an M.D. in her California State, although it's taken her over thirty years to do it. (All those who do mothering in any form undoubtedly recognize how much work goes into obtaining a Mothering Degree.)

Victoria likes goodness, hot bubble baths, people who are kind, white-cheese popcorn, hugs and cute little notes from her great kids, and kisses from her wonderful husband. She is not particularly fond of finding out about massive science projects that are due the next day, gruesome movies, dogs who discover an especially delicious piece of trash that they spread all over the entire living room, and seeing a daughter come home from her friend's house after they decided to play "beauty shop," with one of her ponytails cut off.

Victoria has ten children to whom she personally gave birth, as well as one wonderful bonus son. She and her husband Jay and their last three teenagers live just five minutes away from the beautiful Redlands California Temple.

The Girl in a Whirl by "Dr. Sue," and Other Things that Women Do is Victoria's first book. She would enjoy hearing from her readers at victoriagunther@gmail.com or at her website, girlinawhirl.com.